C-3273 CAREER EXAMINATION SERIES

This is your
PASSBOOK for...

Clerk III

Test Preparation Study Guide
Questions & Answers

COPYRIGHT NOTICE

This book is SOLELY intended for, is sold ONLY to, and its use is RESTRICTED to individual, bona fide applicants or candidates who qualify by virtue of having seriously filed applications for appropriate license, certificate, professional and/or promotional advancement, higher school matriculation, scholarship, or other legitimate requirements of education and/or governmental authorities.

This book is NOT intended for use, class instruction, tutoring, training, duplication, copying, reprinting, excerption, or adaptation, etc., by:

1) Other publishers
2) Proprietors and/or Instructors of "Coaching" and/or Preparatory Courses
3) Personnel and/or Training Divisions of commercial, industrial, and governmental organizations
4) Schools, colleges, or universities and/or their departments and staffs, including teachers and other personnel
5) Testing Agencies or Bureaus
6) Study groups which seek by the purchase of a single volume to copy and/or duplicate and/or adapt this material for use by the group as a whole without having purchased individual volumes for each of the members of the group
7) Et al.

Such persons would be in violation of appropriate Federal and State statutes.

PROVISION OF LICENSING AGREEMENTS – Recognized educational, commercial, industrial, and governmental institutions and organizations, and others legitimately engaged in educational pursuits, including training, testing, and measurement activities, may address request for a licensing agreement to the copyright owners, who will determine whether, and under what conditions, including fees and charges, the materials in this book may be used them. In other words, a licensing facility exists for the legitimate use of the material in this book on other than an individual basis. However, it is asseverated and affirmed here that the material in this book CANNOT be used without the receipt of the express permission of such a licensing agreement from the Publishers. Inquiries re licensing should be addressed to the company, attention rights and permissions department.

All rights reserved, including the right of reproduction in whole or in part, in any form or by any means, electronic or mechanical, including photocopying, recording, or by any information storage and retrieval system, without permission in writing from the Publisher.

Copyright © 2024 by
National Learning Corporation

212 Michael Drive, Syosset, NY 11791
(516) 921-8888 • www.passbooks.com
E-mail: info@passbooks.com

PUBLISHED IN THE UNITED STATES OF AMERICA

PASSBOOK® SERIES

THE *PASSBOOK® SERIES* has been created to prepare applicants and candidates for the ultimate academic battlefield – the examination room.

At some time in our lives, each and every one of us may be required to take an examination – for validation, matriculation, admission, qualification, registration, certification, or licensure.

Based on the assumption that every applicant or candidate has met the basic formal educational standards, has taken the required number of courses, and read the necessary texts, the *PASSBOOK® SERIES* furnishes the one special preparation which may assure passing with confidence, instead of failing with insecurity. Examination questions – together with answers – are furnished as the basic vehicle for study so that the mysteries of the examination and its compounding difficulties may be eliminated or diminished by a sure method.

This book is meant to help you pass your examination provided that you qualify and are serious in your objective.

The entire field is reviewed through the huge store of content information which is succinctly presented through a provocative and challenging approach – the question-and-answer method.

A climate of success is established by furnishing the correct answers at the end of each test.

You soon learn to recognize types of questions, forms of questions, and patterns of questioning. You may even begin to anticipate expected outcomes.

You perceive that many questions are repeated or adapted so that you can gain acute insights, which may enable you to score many sure points.

You learn how to confront new questions, or types of questions, and to attack them confidently and work out the correct answers.

You note objectives and emphases, and recognize pitfalls and dangers, so that you may make positive educational adjustments.

Moreover, you are kept fully informed in relation to new concepts, methods, practices, and directions in the field.

You discover that you are actually taking the examination all the time: you are preparing for the examination by "taking" an examination, not by reading extraneous and/or supererogatory textbooks.

In short, this PASSBOOK®, used directedly, should be an important factor in helping you to pass your test.

CLERK III

DUTIES:
Plans, assigns, and reviews the work of clerical personnel engaged in processing personnel educational, medical, legal documents, or other departmental records. The work involves responsibility for the independent performance of varied clerical duties requiring a moderate degree of decision making. The use of a personal computer for word processing and database entry is an integral part of this position. Duties may involve contact with the general public. The work is performed in accordance with well-defined objectives, policies and procedures, but detailed instructions are given for new or difficult assignments. The work is usually submitted in its final form and is subject to general review by superiors. The employee reports directly to and works under the general supervision of a higher-level employee. Performs related duties as required.

TYPICAL WORK ACTIVITIES:
- Checks items, data or names in files for accuracy and completeness;
- Searches files for information;
- Prepares new file folders;
- Sorts and distributes mail;
- Enters data into a personal computer;
- Answers telephone and obtains and gives out information about office function and services;
- Refers telephone calls to proper office and personnel or takes messages;
- Greets individual visitors and refers them to the proper person;
- Schedules meetings and appointments.

SUBJECT OF EXAMINATION:
The written test designed to evaluate knowledge, skills and /or abilities in the following areas:
1. **Office management** - These questions test for knowledge of the principles and practices of planning, organizing and controlling the activities of an office and directing those performing office activities so as to achieve predetermined objectives such as accomplishing office work within reasonable limits of time, effort and cost expenditure. Typical activities may include but will not be restricted to: simplifying and improving procedures, increasing office efficiency, improving the office work environment and controlling office supplies.
2. **Office record keeping** - These questions test your ability to perform common office record keeping tasks. The test consists of two or more "sets" of questions, each set concerning a different problem. Typical record keeping problems might involve the organization or collation of data from several sources; scheduling; maintaining a record system using running balances; or completion of a table summarizing data using totals, subtotals, averages and percents.
3. **Preparing written material** - These questions test for the ability to present information clearly and accurately, and to organize paragraphs logically and comprehensibly. For some questions, you will be given information in two or three sentences followed by four restatements of the information. You must then choose the best version. For other questions, you will be given paragraphs with their sentences out of order. You must then choose, from four suggestions, the best order for the sentences.

4. **Supervision** - These questions test for knowledge of the principles and practices employed in planning, organizing, and controlling the activities of a work unit toward predetermined objectives. The concepts covered, usually in a situational question format, include such topics as assigning and reviewing work; evaluating performance; maintaining work standards; motivating and developing subordinates; implementing procedural change; increasing efficiency; and dealing with problems of absenteeism, morale, and discipline.
5. **Understanding and interpreting written material** - These questions test for the ability to understand and interpret written material. You will be presented with brief reading passages and will be asked questions about the passages. You should base your answers to the questions only on what is presented in the passages and not on what you may happen to know about the topic.

HOW TO TAKE A TEST

I. YOU MUST PASS AN EXAMINATION

A. WHAT EVERY CANDIDATE SHOULD KNOW

Examination applicants often ask us for help in preparing for the written test. What can I study in advance? What kinds of questions will be asked? How will the test be given? How will the papers be graded?

As an applicant for a civil service examination, you may be wondering about some of these things. Our purpose here is to suggest effective methods of advance study and to describe civil service examinations.

Your chances for success on this examination can be increased if you know how to prepare. Those "pre-examination jitters" can be reduced if you know what to expect. You can even experience an adventure in good citizenship if you know why civil service exams are given.

B. WHY ARE CIVIL SERVICE EXAMINATIONS GIVEN?

Civil service examinations are important to you in two ways. As a citizen, you want public jobs filled by employees who know how to do their work. As a job seeker, you want a fair chance to compete for that job on an equal footing with other candidates. The best-known means of accomplishing this two-fold goal is the competitive examination.

Exams are widely publicized throughout the nation. They may be administered for jobs in federal, state, city, municipal, town or village governments or agencies.

Any citizen may apply, with some limitations, such as the age or residence of applicants. Your experience and education may be reviewed to see whether you meet the requirements for the particular examination. When these requirements exist, they are reasonable and applied consistently to all applicants. Thus, a competitive examination may cause you some uneasiness now, but it is your privilege and safeguard.

C. HOW ARE CIVIL SERVICE EXAMS DEVELOPED?

Examinations are carefully written by trained technicians who are specialists in the field known as "psychological measurement," in consultation with recognized authorities in the field of work that the test will cover. These experts recommend the subject matter areas or skills to be tested; only those knowledges or skills important to your success on the job are included. The most reliable books and source materials available are used as references. Together, the experts and technicians judge the difficulty level of the questions.

Test technicians know how to phrase questions so that the problem is clearly stated. Their ethics do not permit "trick" or "catch" questions. Questions may have been tried out on sample groups, or subjected to statistical analysis, to determine their usefulness.

Written tests are often used in combination with performance tests, ratings of training and experience, and oral interviews. All of these measures combine to form the best-known means of finding the right person for the right job.

II. HOW TO PASS THE WRITTEN TEST

A. NATURE OF THE EXAMINATION

To prepare intelligently for civil service examinations, you should know how they differ from school examinations you have taken. In school you were assigned certain definite pages to read or subjects to cover. The examination questions were quite detailed and usually emphasized memory. Civil service exams, on the other hand, try to discover your present ability to perform the duties of a position, plus your potentiality to learn these duties. In other words, a civil service exam attempts to predict how successful you will be. Questions cover such a broad area that they cannot be as minute and detailed as school exam questions.

In the public service similar kinds of work, or positions, are grouped together in one "class." This process is known as *position-classification*. All the positions in a class are paid according to the salary range for that class. One class title covers all of these positions, and they are all tested by the same examination.

B. FOUR BASIC STEPS

1) Study the announcement

How, then, can you know what subjects to study? Our best answer is: "Learn as much as possible about the class of positions for which you've applied." The exam will test the knowledge, skills and abilities needed to do the work.

Your most valuable source of information about the position you want is the official exam announcement. This announcement lists the training and experience qualifications. Check these standards and apply only if you come reasonably close to meeting them.

The brief description of the position in the examination announcement offers some clues to the subjects which will be tested. Think about the job itself. Review the duties in your mind. Can you perform them, or are there some in which you are rusty? Fill in the blank spots in your preparation.

Many jurisdictions preview the written test in the exam announcement by including a section called "Knowledge and Abilities Required," "Scope of the Examination," or some similar heading. Here you will find out specifically what fields will be tested.

2) Review your own background

Once you learn in general what the position is all about, and what you need to know to do the work, ask yourself which subjects you already know fairly well and which need improvement. You may wonder whether to concentrate on improving your strong areas or on building some background in your fields of weakness. When the announcement has specified "some knowledge" or "considerable knowledge," or has used adjectives like "beginning principles of..." or "advanced ... methods," you can get a clue as to the number and difficulty of questions to be asked in any given field. More questions, and hence broader coverage, would be included for those subjects which are more important in the work. Now weigh your strengths and weaknesses against the job requirements and prepare accordingly.

3) Determine the level of the position

Another way to tell how intensively you should prepare is to understand the level of the job for which you are applying. Is it the entering level? In other words, is this the position in which beginners in a field of work are hired? Or is it an intermediate or advanced level? Sometimes this is indicated by such words as "Junior" or "Senior" in the class title. Other jurisdictions use Roman numerals to designate the level – Clerk I, Clerk II, for example. The word "Supervisor" sometimes appears in the title. If the level is not indicated by the title, check the description of duties. Will you be working under very close supervision, or will you have responsibility for independent decisions in this work?

4) Choose appropriate study materials

Now that you know the subjects to be examined and the relative amount of each subject to be covered, you can choose suitable study materials. For beginning level jobs, or even advanced ones, if you have a pronounced weakness in some aspect of your training, read a modern, standard textbook in that field. Be sure it is up to date and has general coverage. Such books are normally available at your library, and the librarian will be glad to help you locate one. For entry-level positions, questions of appropriate difficulty are chosen – neither highly advanced questions, nor those too simple. Such questions require careful thought but not advanced training.

If the position for which you are applying is technical or advanced, you will read more advanced, specialized material. If you are already familiar with the basic principles of your field, elementary textbooks would waste your time. Concentrate on advanced textbooks and technical periodicals. Think through the concepts and review difficult problems in your field.

These are all general sources. You can get more ideas on your own initiative, following these leads. For example, training manuals and publications of the government agency which employs workers in your field can be useful, particularly for technical and professional positions. A letter or visit to the government department involved may result in more specific study suggestions, and certainly will provide you with a more definite idea of the exact nature of the position you are seeking.

III. KINDS OF TESTS

Tests are used for purposes other than measuring knowledge and ability to perform specified duties. For some positions, it is equally important to test ability to make adjustments to new situations or to profit from training. In others, basic mental abilities not dependent on information are essential. Questions which test these things may not appear as pertinent to the duties of the position as those which test for knowledge and information. Yet they are often highly important parts of a fair examination. For very general questions, it is almost impossible to help you direct your study efforts. What we can do is to point out some of the more common of these general abilities needed in public service positions and describe some typical questions.

1) General information

Broad, general information has been found useful for predicting job success in some kinds of work. This is tested in a variety of ways, from vocabulary lists to questions about current events. Basic background in some field of work, such as sociology or economics, may be sampled in a group of questions. Often these are principles which have become familiar to most persons through exposure rather than through formal training. It is difficult to advise you how to study for these questions; being alert to the world around you is our best suggestion.

2) Verbal ability

An example of an ability needed in many positions is verbal or language ability. Verbal ability is, in brief, the ability to use and understand words. Vocabulary and grammar tests are typical measures of this ability. Reading comprehension or paragraph interpretation questions are common in many kinds of civil service tests. You are given a paragraph of written material and asked to find its central meaning.

3) Numerical ability

Number skills can be tested by the familiar arithmetic problem, by checking paired lists of numbers to see which are alike and which are different, or by interpreting charts and graphs. In the latter test, a graph may be printed in the test booklet which you are asked to use as the basis for answering questions.

4) Observation

A popular test for law-enforcement positions is the observation test. A picture is shown to you for several minutes, then taken away. Questions about the picture test your ability to observe both details and larger elements.

5) Following directions

In many positions in the public service, the employee must be able to carry out written instructions dependably and accurately. You may be given a chart with several columns, each column listing a variety of information. The questions require you to carry out directions involving the information given in the chart.

6) Skills and aptitudes

Performance tests effectively measure some manual skills and aptitudes. When the skill is one in which you are trained, such as typing or shorthand, you can practice. These tests are often very much like those given in business school or high school courses. For many of the other skills and aptitudes, however, no short-time preparation can be made. Skills and abilities natural to you or that you have developed throughout your lifetime are being tested.

Many of the general questions just described provide all the data needed to answer the questions and ask you to use your reasoning ability to find the answers. Your best preparation for these tests, as well as for tests of facts and ideas, is to be at your physical and mental best. You, no doubt, have your own methods of getting into an exam-taking mood and keeping "in shape." The next section lists some ideas on this subject.

IV. KINDS OF QUESTIONS

Only rarely is the "essay" question, which you answer in narrative form, used in civil service tests. Civil service tests are usually of the short-answer type. Full instructions for answering these questions will be given to you at the examination. But in case this is your first experience with short-answer questions and separate answer sheets, here is what you need to know:

1) **Multiple-choice Questions**

Most popular of the short-answer questions is the "multiple choice" or "best answer" question. It can be used, for example, to test for factual knowledge, ability to solve problems or judgment in meeting situations found at work.

A multiple-choice question is normally one of three types—
- It can begin with an incomplete statement followed by several possible endings. You are to find the one ending which *best* completes the statement, although some of the others may not be entirely wrong.
- It can also be a complete statement in the form of a question which is answered by choosing one of the statements listed.

- It can be in the form of a problem – again you select the best answer.

Here is an example of a multiple-choice question with a discussion which should give you some clues as to the method for choosing the right answer:

When an employee has a complaint about his assignment, the action which will *best* help him overcome his difficulty is to
  A. discuss his difficulty with his coworkers
  B. take the problem to the head of the organization
  C. take the problem to the person who gave him the assignment
  D. say nothing to anyone about his complaint

In answering this question, you should study each of the choices to find which is best. Consider choice "A" – Certainly an employee may discuss his complaint with fellow employees, but no change or improvement can result, and the complaint remains unresolved. Choice "B" is a poor choice since the head of the organization probably does not know what assignment you have been given, and taking your problem to him is known as "going over the head" of the supervisor. The supervisor, or person who made the assignment, is the person who can clarify it or correct any injustice. Choice "C" is, therefore, correct. To say nothing, as in choice "D," is unwise. Supervisors have and interest in knowing the problems employees are facing, and the employee is seeking a solution to his problem.

2) True/False Questions

The "true/false" or "right/wrong" form of question is sometimes used. Here a complete statement is given. Your job is to decide whether the statement is right or wrong.

SAMPLE: A roaming cell-phone call to a nearby city costs less than a non-roaming call to a distant city.

This statement is wrong, or false, since roaming calls are more expensive.

This is not a complete list of all possible question forms, although most of the others are variations of these common types. You will always get complete directions for answering questions. Be sure you understand *how* to mark your answers – ask questions until you do.

V. RECORDING YOUR ANSWERS

Computer terminals are used more and more today for many different kinds of exams.

For an examination with very few applicants, you may be told to record your answers in the test booklet itself. Separate answer sheets are much more common. If this separate answer sheet is to be scored by machine – and this is often the case – it is highly important that you mark your answers correctly in order to get credit.

An electronic scoring machine is often used in civil service offices because of the speed with which papers can be scored. Machine-scored answer sheets must be marked with a pencil, which will be given to you. This pencil has a high graphite content which responds to the electronic scoring machine. As a matter of fact, stray dots may register as answers, so do not let your pencil rest on the answer sheet while you are pondering the correct answer. Also, if your pencil lead breaks or is otherwise defective, ask for another.

Since the answer sheet will be dropped in a slot in the scoring machine, be careful not to bend the corners or get the paper crumpled.

The answer sheet normally has five vertical columns of numbers, with 30 numbers to a column. These numbers correspond to the question numbers in your test booklet. After each number, going across the page are four or five pairs of dotted lines. These short dotted lines have small letters or numbers above them. The first two pairs may also have a "T" or "F" above the letters. This indicates that the first two pairs only are to be used if the questions are of the true-false type. If the questions are multiple choice, disregard the "T" and "F" and pay attention only to the small letters or numbers.

Answer your questions in the manner of the sample that follows:

32. The largest city in the United States is
    A. Washington, D.C.
    B. New York City
    C. Chicago
    D. Detroit
    E. San Francisco

1) Choose the answer you think is best. (New York City is the largest, so "B" is correct.)
2) Find the row of dotted lines numbered the same as the question you are answering. (Find row number 32)
3) Find the pair of dotted lines corresponding to the answer. (Find the pair of lines under the mark "B.")
4) Make a solid black mark between the dotted lines.

VI. BEFORE THE TEST

Common sense will help you find procedures to follow to get ready for an examination. Too many of us, however, overlook these sensible measures. Indeed, nervousness and fatigue have been found to be the most serious reasons why applicants fail to do their best on civil service tests. Here is a list of reminders:

- Begin your preparation early – Don't wait until the last minute to go scurrying around for books and materials or to find out what the position is all about.
- Prepare continuously – An hour a night for a week is better than an all-night cram session. This has been definitely established. What is more, a night a week for a month will return better dividends than crowding your study into a shorter period of time.
- Locate the place of the exam – You have been sent a notice telling you when and where to report for the examination. If the location is in a different town or otherwise unfamiliar to you, it would be well to inquire the best route and learn something about the building.
- Relax the night before the test – Allow your mind to rest. Do not study at all that night. Plan some mild recreation or diversion; then go to bed early and get a good night's sleep.
- Get up early enough to make a leisurely trip to the place for the test – This way unforeseen events, traffic snarls, unfamiliar buildings, etc. will not upset you.
- Dress comfortably – A written test is not a fashion show. You will be known by number and not by name, so wear something comfortable.

- Leave excess paraphernalia at home – Shopping bags and odd bundles will get in your way. You need bring only the items mentioned in the official notice you received; usually everything you need is provided. Do not bring reference books to the exam. They will only confuse those last minutes and be taken away from you when in the test room.
- Arrive somewhat ahead of time – If because of transportation schedules you must get there very early, bring a newspaper or magazine to take your mind off yourself while waiting.
- Locate the examination room – When you have found the proper room, you will be directed to the seat or part of the room where you will sit. Sometimes you are given a sheet of instructions to read while you are waiting. Do not fill out any forms until you are told to do so; just read them and be prepared.
- Relax and prepare to listen to the instructions
- If you have any physical problem that may keep you from doing your best, be sure to tell the test administrator. If you are sick or in poor health, you really cannot do your best on the exam. You can come back and take the test some other time.

VII. AT THE TEST

The day of the test is here and you have the test booklet in your hand. The temptation to get going is very strong. Caution! There is more to success than knowing the right answers. You must know how to identify your papers and understand variations in the type of short-answer question used in this particular examination. Follow these suggestions for maximum results from your efforts:

1) Cooperate with the monitor

The test administrator has a duty to create a situation in which you can be as much at ease as possible. He will give instructions, tell you when to begin, check to see that you are marking your answer sheet correctly, and so on. He is not there to guard you, although he will see that your competitors do not take unfair advantage. He wants to help you do your best.

2) Listen to all instructions

Don't jump the gun! Wait until you understand all directions. In most civil service tests you get more time than you need to answer the questions. So don't be in a hurry. Read each word of instructions until you clearly understand the meaning. Study the examples, listen to all announcements and follow directions. Ask questions if you do not understand what to do.

3) Identify your papers

Civil service exams are usually identified by number only. You will be assigned a number; you must not put your name on your test papers. Be sure to copy your number correctly. Since more than one exam may be given, copy your exact examination title.

4) Plan your time

Unless you are told that a test is a "speed" or "rate of work" test, speed itself is usually not important. Time enough to answer all the questions will be provided, but this does not mean that you have all day. An overall time limit has been set. Divide the total time (in minutes) by the number of questions to determine the approximate time you have for each question.

5) Do not linger over difficult questions

If you come across a difficult question, mark it with a paper clip (useful to have along) and come back to it when you have been through the booklet. One caution if you do this – be sure to skip a number on your answer sheet as well. Check often to be sure that you have not lost your place and that you are marking in the row numbered the same as the question you are answering.

6) Read the questions

Be sure you know what the question asks! Many capable people are unsuccessful because they failed to *read* the questions correctly.

7) Answer all questions

Unless you have been instructed that a penalty will be deducted for incorrect answers, it is better to guess than to omit a question.

8) Speed tests

It is often better NOT to guess on speed tests. It has been found that on timed tests people are tempted to spend the last few seconds before time is called in marking answers at random – without even reading them – in the hope of picking up a few extra points. To discourage this practice, the instructions may warn you that your score will be "corrected" for guessing. That is, a penalty will be applied. The incorrect answers will be deducted from the correct ones, or some other penalty formula will be used.

9) Review your answers

If you finish before time is called, go back to the questions you guessed or omitted to give them further thought. Review other answers if you have time.

10) Return your test materials

If you are ready to leave before others have finished or time is called, take ALL your materials to the monitor and leave quietly. Never take any test material with you. The monitor can discover whose papers are not complete, and taking a test booklet may be grounds for disqualification.

VIII. EXAMINATION TECHNIQUES

1) Read the general instructions carefully. These are usually printed on the first page of the exam booklet. As a rule, these instructions refer to the timing of the examination; the fact that you should not start work until the signal and must stop work at a signal, etc. If there are any *special* instructions, such as a choice of questions to be answered, make sure that you note this instruction carefully.

2) When you are ready to start work on the examination, that is as soon as the signal has been given, read the instructions to each question booklet, underline any key words or phrases, such as *least, best, outline, describe* and the like. In this way you will tend to answer as requested rather than discover on reviewing your paper that you *listed without describing*, that you selected the *worst* choice rather than the *best* choice, etc.

3) If the examination is of the objective or multiple-choice type – that is, each question will also give a series of possible answers: A, B, C or D, and you are called upon to select the best answer and write the letter next to that answer on your answer paper – it is advisable to start answering each question in turn. There may be anywhere from 50 to 100 such questions in the three or four hours allotted and you can see how much time would be taken if you read through all the questions before beginning to answer any. Furthermore, if you come across a question or group of questions which you know would be difficult to answer, it would undoubtedly affect your handling of all the other questions.

4) If the examination is of the essay type and contains but a few questions, it is a moot point as to whether you should read all the questions before starting to answer any one. Of course, if you are given a choice – say five out of seven and the like – then it is essential to read all the questions so you can eliminate the two that are most difficult. If, however, you are asked to answer all the questions, there may be danger in trying to answer the easiest one first because you may find that you will spend too much time on it. The best technique is to answer the first question, then proceed to the second, etc.

5) Time your answers. Before the exam begins, write down the time it started, then add the time allowed for the examination and write down the time it must be completed, then divide the time available somewhat as follows:
    - If 3-1/2 hours are allowed, that would be 210 minutes. If you have 80 objective-type questions, that would be an average of 2-1/2 minutes per question. Allow yourself no more than 2 minutes per question, or a total of 160 minutes, which will permit about 50 minutes to review.
    - If for the time allotment of 210 minutes there are 7 essay questions to answer, that would average about 30 minutes a question. Give yourself only 25 minutes per question so that you have about 35 minutes to review.

6) The most important instruction is to *read each question* and make sure you know what is wanted. The second most important instruction is to *time yourself properly* so that you answer every question. The third most important instruction is to *answer every question*. Guess if you have to but include something for each question. Remember that you will receive no credit for a blank and will probably receive some credit if you write something in answer to an essay question. If you guess a letter – say "B" for a multiple-choice question – you may have guessed right. If you leave a blank as an answer to a multiple-choice question, the examiners may respect your feelings but it will not add a point to your score. Some exams may penalize you for wrong answers, so in such cases *only*, you may not want to guess unless you have some basis for your answer.

7) Suggestions
    a. Objective-type questions
        1. Examine the question booklet for proper sequence of pages and questions
        2. Read all instructions carefully
        3. Skip any question which seems too difficult; return to it after all other questions have been answered
        4. Apportion your time properly; do not spend too much time on any single question or group of questions

5. Note and underline key words – *all, most, fewest, least, best, worst, same, opposite*, etc.
6. Pay particular attention to negatives
7. Note unusual option, e.g., unduly long, short, complex, different or similar in content to the body of the question
8. Observe the use of "hedging" words – *probably, may, most likely*, etc.
9. Make sure that your answer is put next to the same number as the question
10. Do not second-guess unless you have good reason to believe the second answer is definitely more correct
11. Cross out original answer if you decide another answer is more accurate; do not erase until you are ready to hand your paper in
12. Answer all questions; guess unless instructed otherwise
13. Leave time for review

   b. Essay questions
     1. Read each question carefully
     2. Determine exactly what is wanted. Underline key words or phrases.
     3. Decide on outline or paragraph answer
     4. Include many different points and elements unless asked to develop any one or two points or elements
     5. Show impartiality by giving pros and cons unless directed to select one side only
     6. Make and write down any assumptions you find necessary to answer the questions
     7. Watch your English, grammar, punctuation and choice of words
     8. Time your answers; don't crowd material

8) Answering the essay question

Most essay questions can be answered by framing the specific response around several key words or ideas. Here are a few such key words or ideas:

M's: manpower, materials, methods, money, management
P's: purpose, program, policy, plan, procedure, practice, problems, pitfalls, personnel, public relations

   a. Six basic steps in handling problems:
     1. Preliminary plan and background development
     2. Collect information, data and facts
     3. Analyze and interpret information, data and facts
     4. Analyze and develop solutions as well as make recommendations
     5. Prepare report and sell recommendations
     6. Install recommendations and follow up effectiveness

   b. Pitfalls to avoid
     1. *Taking things for granted* – A statement of the situation does not necessarily imply that each of the elements is necessarily true; for example, a complaint may be invalid and biased so that all that can be taken for granted is that a complaint has been registered

2. *Considering only one side of a situation* – Wherever possible, indicate several alternatives and then point out the reasons you selected the best one
3. *Failing to indicate follow up* – Whenever your answer indicates action on your part, make certain that you will take proper follow-up action to see how successful your recommendations, procedures or actions turn out to be
4. *Taking too long in answering any single question* – Remember to time your answers properly

IX. AFTER THE TEST

Scoring procedures differ in detail among civil service jurisdictions although the general principles are the same. Whether the papers are hand-scored or graded by machine we have described, they are nearly always graded by number. That is, the person who marks the paper knows only the number – never the name – of the applicant. Not until all the papers have been graded will they be matched with names. If other tests, such as training and experience or oral interview ratings have been given, scores will be combined. Different parts of the examination usually have different weights. For example, the written test might count 60 percent of the final grade, and a rating of training and experience 40 percent. In many jurisdictions, veterans will have a certain number of points added to their grades.

After the final grade has been determined, the names are placed in grade order and an eligible list is established. There are various methods for resolving ties between those who get the same final grade – probably the most common is to place first the name of the person whose application was received first. Job offers are made from the eligible list in the order the names appear on it. You will be notified of your grade and your rank as soon as all these computations have been made. This will be done as rapidly as possible.

People who are found to meet the requirements in the announcement are called "eligibles." Their names are put on a list of eligible candidates. An eligible's chances of getting a job depend on how high he stands on this list and how fast agencies are filling jobs from the list.

When a job is to be filled from a list of eligibles, the agency asks for the names of people on the list of eligibles for that job. When the civil service commission receives this request, it sends to the agency the names of the three people highest on this list. Or, if the job to be filled has specialized requirements, the office sends the agency the names of the top three persons who meet these requirements from the general list.

The appointing officer makes a choice from among the three people whose names were sent to him. If the selected person accepts the appointment, the names of the others are put back on the list to be considered for future openings.

That is the rule in hiring from all kinds of eligible lists, whether they are for typist, carpenter, chemist, or something else. For every vacancy, the appointing officer has his choice of any one of the top three eligibles on the list. This explains why the person whose name is on top of the list sometimes does not get an appointment when some of the persons lower on the list do. If the appointing officer chooses the second or third eligible, the No. 1 eligible does not get a job at once, but stays on the list until he is appointed or the list is terminated.

X. HOW TO PASS THE INTERVIEW TEST

The examination for which you applied requires an oral interview test. You have already taken the written test and you are now being called for the interview test – the final part of the formal examination.

You may think that it is not possible to prepare for an interview test and that there are no procedures to follow during an interview. Our purpose is to point out some things you can do in advance that will help you and some good rules to follow and pitfalls to avoid while you are being interviewed.

What is an interview supposed to test?

The written examination is designed to test the technical knowledge and competence of the candidate; the oral is designed to evaluate intangible qualities, not readily measured otherwise, and to establish a list showing the relative fitness of each candidate – as measured against his competitors – for the position sought. Scoring is not on the basis of "right" and "wrong," but on a sliding scale of values ranging from "not passable" to "outstanding." As a matter of fact, it is possible to achieve a relatively low score without a single "incorrect" answer because of evident weakness in the qualities being measured.

Occasionally, an examination may consist entirely of an oral test – either an individual or a group oral. In such cases, information is sought concerning the technical knowledges and abilities of the candidate, since there has been no written examination for this purpose. More commonly, however, an oral test is used to supplement a written examination.

Who conducts interviews?

The composition of oral boards varies among different jurisdictions. In nearly all, a representative of the personnel department serves as chairman. One of the members of the board may be a representative of the department in which the candidate would work. In some cases, "outside experts" are used, and, frequently, a businessman or some other representative of the general public is asked to serve. Labor and management or other special groups may be represented. The aim is to secure the services of experts in the appropriate field.

However the board is composed, it is a good idea (and not at all improper or unethical) to ascertain in advance of the interview who the members are and what groups they represent. When you are introduced to them, you will have some idea of their backgrounds and interests, and at least you will not stutter and stammer over their names.

What should be done before the interview?

While knowledge about the board members is useful and takes some of the surprise element out of the interview, there is other preparation which is more substantive. It *is* possible to prepare for an oral interview – in several ways:

1) Keep a copy of your application and review it carefully before the interview

This may be the only document before the oral board, and the starting point of the interview. Know what education and experience you have listed there, and the sequence and dates of all of it. Sometimes the board will ask you to review the highlights of your experience for them; you should not have to hem and haw doing it.

2) Study the class specification and the examination announcement

Usually, the oral board has one or both of these to guide them. The qualities, characteristics or knowledges required by the position sought are stated in these documents. They offer valuable clues as to the nature of the oral interview. For example, if the job involves supervisory responsibilities, the announcement will usually indicate that knowledge of modern supervisory methods and the qualifications of the candidate as a supervisor will be tested. If so, you can expect such questions, frequently in the form of a hypothetical situation which you are expected to solve. NEVER go into an oral without knowledge of the duties and responsibilities of the job you seek.

3) Think through each qualification required

Try to visualize the kind of questions you would ask if you were a board member. How well could you answer them? Try especially to appraise your own knowledge and background in each area, *measured against the job sought*, and identify any areas in which you are weak. Be critical and realistic – do not flatter yourself.

4) Do some general reading in areas in which you feel you may be weak

For example, if the job involves supervision and your past experience has NOT, some general reading in supervisory methods and practices, particularly in the field of human relations, might be useful. Do NOT study agency procedures or detailed manuals. The oral board will be testing your understanding and capacity, not your memory.

5) Get a good night's sleep and watch your general health and mental attitude

You will want a clear head at the interview. Take care of a cold or any other minor ailment, and of course, no hangovers.

What should be done on the day of the interview?

Now comes the day of the interview itself. Give yourself plenty of time to get there. Plan to arrive somewhat ahead of the scheduled time, particularly if your appointment is in the fore part of the day. If a previous candidate fails to appear, the board might be ready for you a bit early. By early afternoon an oral board is almost invariably behind schedule if there are many candidates, and you may have to wait. Take along a book or magazine to read, or your application to review, but leave any extraneous material in the waiting room when you go in for your interview. In any event, relax and compose yourself.

The matter of dress is important. The board is forming impressions about you – from your experience, your manners, your attitude, and your appearance. Give your personal appearance careful attention. Dress your best, but not your flashiest. Choose conservative, appropriate clothing, and be sure it is immaculate. This is a business interview, and your appearance should indicate that you regard it as such. Besides, being well groomed and properly dressed will help boost your confidence.

Sooner or later, someone will call your name and escort you into the interview room. *This is it.* From here on you are on your own. It is too late for any more preparation. But remember, you asked for this opportunity to prove your fitness, and you are here because your request was granted.

What happens when you go in?

The usual sequence of events will be as follows: The clerk (who is often the board stenographer) will introduce you to the chairman of the oral board, who will introduce you to the other members of the board. Acknowledge the introductions before you sit down. Do not be surprised if you find a microphone facing you or a stenotypist sitting by. Oral interviews are usually recorded in the event of an appeal or other review.

Usually the chairman of the board will open the interview by reviewing the highlights of your education and work experience from your application – primarily for the benefit of the other members of the board, as well as to get the material into the record. Do not interrupt or comment unless there is an error or significant misinterpretation; if that is the case, do not hesitate. But do not quibble about insignificant matters. Also, he will usually ask you some question about your education, experience or your present job – partly to get you to start talking and to establish the interviewing "rapport." He may start the actual questioning, or turn it over to one of the other members. Frequently, each member undertakes the questioning on a particular area, one in which he is perhaps most competent, so you can expect each member to participate in the examination. Because time is limited, you may also expect some rather abrupt switches in the direction the questioning takes, so do not be upset by it. Normally, a board member will not pursue a single line of questioning unless he discovers a particular strength or weakness.

After each member has participated, the chairman will usually ask whether any member has any further questions, then will ask you if you have anything you wish to add. Unless you are expecting this question, it may floor you. Worse, it may start you off on an extended, extemporaneous speech. The board is not usually seeking more information. The question is principally to offer you a last opportunity to present further qualifications or to indicate that you have nothing to add. So, if you feel that a significant qualification or characteristic has been overlooked, it is proper to point it out in a sentence or so. Do not compliment the board on the thoroughness of their examination – they have been sketchy, and you know it. If you wish, merely say, "No thank you, I have nothing further to add." This is a point where you can "talk yourself out" of a good impression or fail to present an important bit of information. Remember, *you close the interview yourself.*

The chairman will then say, "That is all, Mr. _____, thank you." Do not be startled; the interview is over, and quicker than you think. Thank him, gather your belongings and take your leave. Save your sigh of relief for the other side of the door.

How to put your best foot forward

Throughout this entire process, you may feel that the board individually and collectively is trying to pierce your defenses, seek out your hidden weaknesses and embarrass and confuse you. Actually, this is not true. They are obliged to make an appraisal of your qualifications for the job you are seeking, and they want to see you in your best light. Remember, they must interview all candidates and a non-cooperative candidate may become a failure in spite of their best efforts to bring out his qualifications. Here are 15 suggestions that will help you:

1) Be natural – Keep your attitude confident, not cocky

If you are not confident that you can do the job, do not expect the board to be. Do not apologize for your weaknesses, try to bring out your strong points. The board is interested in a positive, not negative, presentation. Cockiness will antagonize any board member and make him wonder if you are covering up a weakness by a false show of strength.

2) Get comfortable, but don't lounge or sprawl

Sit erectly but not stiffly. A careless posture may lead the board to conclude that you are careless in other things, or at least that you are not impressed by the importance of the occasion. Either conclusion is natural, even if incorrect. Do not fuss with your clothing, a pencil or an ashtray. Your hands may occasionally be useful to emphasize a point; do not let them become a point of distraction.

3) Do not wisecrack or make small talk

This is a serious situation, and your attitude should show that you consider it as such. Further, the time of the board is limited – they do not want to waste it, and neither should you.

4) Do not exaggerate your experience or abilities

In the first place, from information in the application or other interviews and sources, the board may know more about you than you think. Secondly, you probably will not get away with it. An experienced board is rather adept at spotting such a situation, so do not take the chance.

5) If you know a board member, do not make a point of it, yet do not hide it

Certainly you are not fooling him, and probably not the other members of the board. Do not try to take advantage of your acquaintanceship – it will probably do you little good.

6) Do not dominate the interview

Let the board do that. They will give you the clues – do not assume that you have to do all the talking. Realize that the board has a number of questions to ask you, and do not try to take up all the interview time by showing off your extensive knowledge of the answer to the first one.

7) Be attentive

You only have 20 minutes or so, and you should keep your attention at its sharpest throughout. When a member is addressing a problem or question to you, give him your undivided attention. Address your reply principally to him, but do not exclude the other board members.

8) Do not interrupt

A board member may be stating a problem for you to analyze. He will ask you a question when the time comes. Let him state the problem, and wait for the question.

9) Make sure you understand the question

Do not try to answer until you are sure what the question is. If it is not clear, restate it in your own words or ask the board member to clarify it for you. However, do not haggle about minor elements.

10) Reply promptly but not hastily

A common entry on oral board rating sheets is "candidate responded readily," or "candidate hesitated in replies." Respond as promptly and quickly as you can, but do not jump to a hasty, ill-considered answer.

11) Do not be peremptory in your answers

A brief answer is proper – but do not fire your answer back. That is a losing game from your point of view. The board member can probably ask questions much faster than you can answer them.

12) Do not try to create the answer you think the board member wants

He is interested in what kind of mind you have and how it works – not in playing games. Furthermore, he can usually spot this practice and will actually grade you down on it.

13) Do not switch sides in your reply merely to agree with a board member

Frequently, a member will take a contrary position merely to draw you out and to see if you are willing and able to defend your point of view. Do not start a debate, yet do not surrender a good position. If a position is worth taking, it is worth defending.

14) Do not be afraid to admit an error in judgment if you are shown to be wrong

The board knows that you are forced to reply without any opportunity for careful consideration. Your answer may be demonstrably wrong. If so, admit it and get on with the interview.

15) Do not dwell at length on your present job

The opening question may relate to your present assignment. Answer the question but do not go into an extended discussion. You are being examined for a *new* job, not your present one. As a matter of fact, try to phrase ALL your answers in terms of the job for which you are being examined.

Basis of Rating

Probably you will forget most of these "do's" and "don'ts" when you walk into the oral interview room. Even remembering them all will not ensure you a passing grade. Perhaps you did not have the qualifications in the first place. But remembering them will help you to put your best foot forward, without treading on the toes of the board members.

Rumor and popular opinion to the contrary notwithstanding, an oral board wants you to make the best appearance possible. They know you are under pressure – but they also want to see how you respond to it as a guide to what your reaction would be under the pressures of the job you seek. They will be influenced by the degree of poise you display, the personal traits you show and the manner in which you respond.

ABOUT THIS BOOK

This book contains tests divided into Examination Sections. Go through each test, answering every question in the margin. We have also attached a sample answer sheet at the back of the book that can be removed and used. At the end of each test look at the answer key and check your answers. On the ones you got wrong, look at the right answer choice and learn. Do not fill in the answers first. Do not memorize the questions and answers, but understand the answer and principles involved. On your test, the questions will likely be different from the samples. Questions are changed and new ones added. If you understand these past questions you should have success with any changes that arise. Tests may consist of several types of questions. We have additional books on each subject should more study be advisable or necessary for you. Finally, the more you study, the better prepared you will be. This book is intended to be the last thing you study before you walk into the examination room. Prior study of relevant texts is also recommended. NLC publishes some of these in our Fundamental Series. Knowledge and good sense are important factors in passing your exam. Good luck also helps. So now study this Passbook, absorb the material contained within and take that knowledge into the examination. Then do your best to pass that exam.

EXAMINATION SECTION

EXAMINATION SECTION
TEST 1

DIRECTIONS: Each question or incomplete statement is followed by several suggested answers or completions. Select the one that BEST answers the question or completes the statement. *PRINT THE LETTER OF THE CORRECT ANSWER IN THE SPACE AT THE RIGHT.*

Questions 1-4.

DIRECTIONS: Questions 1 through 4 are to be answered SOLELY on the basis of the following passage.

Job analysis combined with performance appraisal is an excellent method of determining training needs of individuals. The steps in this method are to determine the specific duties of the job, to evaluate the adequacy with which the employee performs each of these duties, and finally to determine what significant improvements can be made by training.

The list of duties can be obtained in a number of ways: asking the employee, asking the supervisor, observing the employee, etc. Adequacy of performance can be estimated by the employee, but the supervisor's evaluation must also be obtained. This evaluation will usually be based on observation.

What does the supervisor observe? The employee, while he is working; the employee's work relationships; the ease, speed, and sureness of the employee's actions; the way he applies himself to the job; the accuracy and amount of completed work; its conformity with established procedures and standards; the appearance of the work; the soundness of judgment it shows; and, finally, signs of good or poor communication, understanding, and cooperation among employees.

Such observation is a normal and inseparable part of the everyday job of supervision. Systematically, recorded, evaluated, and summarized, it highlights both general and individual training needs.

1. According to the passage, job analysis may be used by the supervisor in 1.____
    A. increasing his own understanding of tasks performed in his unit
    B. increasing efficiency of communication within the organization
    C. assisting personnel experts in the classification of positions
    D. determining in which areas an employee needs more instruction

2. According to the passage, the FIRST step in determining the training needs of employees is to 2.____
    A. locate the significant improvements that can be made by training
    B. determine the specific duties required in a job
    C. evaluate the employee's performance
    D. motivate the employee to want to improve himself

3. On the basis of the above passage, which of the following is the BEST way for a supervisor to determine the adequacy of employee performance?
   A. Check the accuracy and amount of completed work
   B. Ask the training officer
   C. Observe all aspects of the employee's work
   D. Obtain the employee's own estimate

4. Which of the following is NOT mentioned by the passage as a factor to be taken into consideration in judging the adequacy of employee performance?
   A. Accuracy of completed work
   B. Appearance of completed work
   C. Cooperation among employees
   D. Attitude of the employee toward his supervisor

5. In indexing names of business firms and other organizations, ONE of the rules to be followed is:
   A. The word *and* is considered an indexing unit.
   B. When a firm name includes the full name of a person who is not well-known, the person's first name is considered as the first indexing unit.
   C. Usually the units in a firm name are indexed in the order in which they are written.
   D. When a firm's name is made up of single letters (such as ABC Corp.), the letters taken together are considered more than one indexing unit.

6. Assume that people often come to your office with complaints of errors in your agency's handling of their clients. The employees in your office have the job of listening to these complaints and investigating them. One day, when it is almost closing time, a person comes into your office, apparently very angry, and demands that you take care of his complaint at once.
   Your IMMEDIATE reaction should be to
   A. suggest that he return the following day
   B. find out his name and the nature of his complaint
   C. tell him to write a letter
   D. call over your supervisor

7. Assume that part of your job is to notify people concerning whether their applications for a certain program have been approved or disapproved. However, you do not actually make the decision on approval or disapproval. One day, you answer a telephone call from a woman who states that she has not yet received any word on her application. She goes on to tell you her qualifications for the program. From what she has said, you know that persons with such qualifications are usually approved.
   Of the following, which one is the BEST thing for you to say to her?
   A. "You probably will be accepted, but wait until you receive a letter before trying to join the program."
   B. "Since you seem well qualified, I am sure that your application will be approved."

C. "If you can write us a letter emphasizing your qualifications, it may speed up the process."
D. "You will be notified of the results of your application as soon as a decision has been made."

8. Suppose that one of your duties includes answering specific telephone inquiries. Your superior refers a call to you from an irate person who claims that your agency is inefficient and is wasting taxpayers' money.
   Of the following, the BEST way to handle such a call is to
   A. listen briefly and then hang up without answering
   B. note the caller's comments and tell him that you will transmit them to your superiors
   C. connect the caller with the head of your agency
   D. discuss your own opinions with the caller

9. An employee has been assigned to open her division head's mail and place it on his desk. One day, the employee opens a letter which she then notices is marked *Personal*.
   Of the following, the BEST action for her to take is to
   A. write *Personal* on the letter and staple the envelope to the back of the letter
   B. ignore the matter and treat the letter the same way as the others
   C. give it to another division head to hold until her own division head comes into the office
   D. leave the letter in the envelope and write *Sorry opened by mistake* on the envelope and initial it

Questions 10-14.

DIRECTIONS: Questions 10 through 14 each consist of a quotation which contains one word that is incorrectly used because it is not in keeping with the meaning that the quotation is evidently intended to convey. Of the words underlined in each quotation, determine which word is incorrectly used. Then select from among the words lettered A, B, C, and D the word which, when substituted for the incorrectly used word, would BEST help to convey the meaning of the quotation. (Do not indicate a change for an underlined word unless the underlined word is incorrectly used.)

10. Unless reasonable managerial supervision is <u>exercised</u> over office supplies, it is certain that there will be extravagance, <u>rejected</u> items out of stock, <u>excessive</u> prices paid for certain items, and <u>obsolete</u> material in the stockroom.
    A. overlooked   B. immoderate   C. needed   D. instituted

11. Since <u>office</u> supplies are in such <u>common</u> use, an attitude of indifference about their handling is not <u>unusual</u>. Their importance is often recognized only when they are <u>utilized</u> or out of stock, for office employees must have proper supplies if maximum productivity is to be <u>attained</u>.
    A. plentiful   B. unavailable   C. reduced   D. expected

12. Anyone <u>effected</u> by paperwork, <u>interested</u> in or engaged in office work, or desiring to improve <u>informational</u> activities can find materials <u>keyed</u> to his needs.
    A. attentive B. available C. affected D. ambitious

13. Information is <u>homogeneous</u> and must therefore be properly classified so that each type may be <u>employed</u> in ways <u>appropriate</u> to its <u>own peculiar</u> properties.
    A. apparent
    B. heterogeneous
    C. consistent
    D. idiosyncratic

14. <u>Intellectual</u> training may seem a <u>formidable</u> phrase, but it means nothing more than the <u>deliberate</u> cultivation of the ability to think, and there is no <u>dark</u> contrast between the intellectual and the practical.
    A. subjective B. objective C. sharp D. vocational

15. The MOST important reason for having a filing system is to
    A. get papers out of the way
    B. have a record of everything that has happened
    C. retain information to justify your actions
    D. enable rapid retrieval of information

16. The system of filing which is used MOST frequently is called _____ filing.
    A. alphabetic
    B. alphanumeric
    C. geographic
    D. numeric

17. One of the clerks under your supervision has been telephoning frequently to tell you that he was taking the day off. Unless there is a real need for it, taking leave which is not scheduled is frowned upon because it upsets the work schedule.
    Under these circumstances, which of the following reasons for taking the day off is MOST acceptable?
    A. "I can't work when my arthritis bothers me."
    B. "I've been pressured with work from my night job and needed the extra time to catch up."
    C. "My family just moved to a new house, and I needed the time to start the repairs."
    D. "Work here has not been challenging, and I've been looking for another job."

18. One of the employees under your supervision, previously a very satisfactory worker, has begun arriving late one or two mornings each week. No explanation has been offered for this change. You call her to your office for a conference. As you are explaining the purpose of the conference and your need to understand this sudden lateness problem, she becomes very angry and states that you have no right to question her.
    Of the following, the BEST course of action for you to take at this point is to

A. inform her in your most authoritarian tone that you are the supervisor and that you have every right to question her
B. end the conference and advise the employee that you will have no further discussion with her until she controls her temper
C. remain calm, try to calm her down, and when she has quieted, explain the reasons for your questions and the need for answers
D. hold your temper; when she has calmed down, tell her that you will not have a tardy worker in your unit and will have her transferred at once

19. Assume that, in the branch of the agency for which you work, you are the only clerical person on the staff with a supervisory title and, in addition, that you are the office manager. On a particular day when all members of the professional staff are away from the building attending an important meeting, an urgent call comes through requesting some confidential information ordinarily released only by professional staff.
Of the following, the MOST reasonable action for you to take is to
    A. decline to give the information because you are not a member of the professional staff
    B. offer to call back after you get permission from the agency director at the main office
    C. advise the caller that you will supply the information as soon as your chief returns
    D. supply the information requested and inform your chief when she returns

20. As a supervisor, you are scheduled to attend an important conference with your superior. However, that day you learn that your very capable assistant is ill and unable to come to work. Several highly sensitive tasks are scheduled for completion on this day.
Of the following, the BEST way to handle this situation is to
    A. tell your supervisor you cannot attend the meeting and ask that it be postponed
    B. assign one of your staff to see that the jobs are completed and turned in
    C. advise your supervisor of the situation and ask what you should do
    D. call the departments for which the work is being done and ask for an extension of time

21. When a decision needs to be made which is likely to affect units other than his own, a supervisor should USUALLY
    A. make such a decision quickly and then discuss it with his supervisor
    B. make such a decision only after careful consultation with his subordinates
    C. discuss the problem with his immediate superior before making such a decision
    D. have his subordinates arrive at such a decision in conference with the subordinates in the other units

22. Assume that, as a supervisor in Division X, you are training Ms. Y, a new employee, to answer the telephone properly.
You should explain that the BEST way to answer is to pick up the receiver and say:

A. "What is your name, please?" B. "May I help you?"
C. "Ms. Y speaking." D. "Division X, Ms. Y speaking."

Questions 23-25.

DIRECTIONS: Questions 23 through 25 consist of sentences in which two words are missing. Examine each sentence, and then choose from below it the words which should be inserted in the blank spaces in order to create a coherent and well-written sentence.

23. Human behavior is far _____ variable, and therefore _____ predictable, than that of any other species.   23._____
    A. less; as   B. less; not   C. more; not   D. more; less

24. The _____ limitation of this method is that the results are based _____ a narrow sample.   24._____
    A. chief; with   B. chief; on   C. only; for   D. only; to

25. Although there _____ a standard procedure for handling these problems, each case often has _____ own unique features.   25._____
    A. are; its   B. are; their   C. is; its   D. is; their

KEY (CORRECT ANSWERS)

1.	D	11.	B
2.	B	12.	C
3.	C	13.	B
4.	D	14.	C
5.	C	15.	D
6.	B	16.	A
7.	D	17.	A
8.	B	18.	C
9.	D	19.	B
10.	C	20.	C

21. C
22. D
23. D
24. B
25. C

TEST 2

DIRECTIONS: Each question or incomplete statement is followed by several suggested answers or completions. Select the one that BEST answers the question or completes the statement. *PRINT THE LETTER OF THE CORRECT ANSWER IN THE SPACE AT THE RIGHT.*

Questions 1-3.

DIRECTIONS: Questions 1 through 3 each consist of a group of four sentences. Read each sentence carefully, and select the one of the four in each group which represents the BEST English usage for business letters and reports.

1. A. The chairman himself, rather than his aides, has reviewed the report. 1.____
   B. The chairman himself, rather than his aides, have reviewed the report.
   C. The chairmen, not the aide, has reviewed the report.
   D. The aide, not the chairmen, have reviewed the report.

2. A. Various proposals were submitted but the decision is not been made. 2.____
   B. Various proposals has been submitted but the decision has not been made.
   C. Various proposals were submitted but the decision is not been made.
   D. Various proposals have been submitted but the decision has not been made.

3. A. Everyone were rewarded for his successful attempt. 3.____
   B. They were successful in their attempts and each of them was rewarded.
   C. Each of them are rewarded for their successful attempts.
   D. The reward for their successful attempts were made to each of them.

4. Which of the following is MOST suited to arrangement in chronological order? 4.____
   A. Applications for various types and levels of jobs
   B. Issues of a weekly publication
   C. Weekly time cards for all employees for the week of April 21
   D. Personnel records for all employees

5. Words that are *synonymous* with a given word ALWAYS _____ the given word. 5.____
   A. have the same meaning as   B. have the same pronunciation as
   C. have the opposite meaning of   D. can be rhymed with

Questions 6-11.

DIRECTIONS: Questions 6 through 11 are to be answered on the basis of the following chart showing numbers of errors made by four clerks in one work unit for a half-year period.

	Allan	Barry	Cary	David
July	5	4	1	7
August	8	3	9	8
September	7	8	7	5
October	3	6	5	3
November	2	4	4	6
December	5	2	8	4

6. The clerk with the HIGHEST number of errors for the six-month period was
    A. Allan   B. Barry   C. Cary   D. David

6.____

7. If the number of errors made by Allan in the six months shown represented one-eighth of the total errors made by the unit during the entire year, what was the TOTAL number of errors made by the unit for the year?
    A. 124   B. 180   C. 240   D. 360

7.____

8. The number of errors made by David in November was what FRACTION of the total errors made in November?
    A. 1/3   B. 1/6   C. 3/8   D. 3/16

8.____

9. The average number of errors made per month per clerk was MOST NEARLY
    A. 4   B. 5   C. 6   D. 7

9.____

10. Of the total number of errors made during the six-month period, the percentage made in August was MOST NEARLY
    A. 2%   B. 4%   C. 23%   D. 4%

10.____

11. If the number of errors in the unit were to decrease in the next six months by 30%, what would be MOST NEARLY the total number of errors for the unit for the next six months?
    A. 87   B. 94   C. 120   D. 137

11.____

12. The arithmetic mean salary for five employees earning $18,500, $18,300, $18,600, $18,400, and $18,500, respectively is
    A. $18,450   B. $18,460   C. $18,475   D. $18,500

12.____

13. Last year, a city department which is responsible for purchasing supplies ordered bond paper in equal quantities from 22 different companies. The price was exactly the same for each company, and the total cost for the 22 orders was $693,113.
Assuming prices did not change during the year, the cost of EACH order was MOST NEARLY
    A. $31,490   B. $31,495   C. $31,500   D. $31,505

13.____

14. A city agency engaged in repair work uses a small part which the city purchases for $0.14 each. Assume that, in a certain year, the total expenditure of the city for this part was $700.
    How MANY of these parts were purchased that year?
    A. 50   B. 200   C. 2,000   D. 5,000

15. The work unit which you supervise is responsible for processing fifteen reports per month.
    If your unit has four clerks and the best worker completes 40% of the reports himself, how many reports would each of the other clerks have to complete if they all do an equal number?
    A. 1   B. 2   C. 3   D. 4

16. Assume that the work unit in which you work has 24 clerks and 18 stenographers. In order to change the ratio of stenographers to clerks so that there is one stenographer for every four clerks, it would be necessary to REDUCE the number of stenographers by
    A. 3   B. 6   C. 9   D. 12

17. Assume that your office is responsible for opening and distributing all the mail of the division. After opening a letter, one of your subordinates notices that it states that there should be an enclosure in the envelope. However, there is no enclosure in the envelope.
    Of the following, the BEST instruction that you can give the clerk is to
    A. call the sender to obtain the enclosure
    B. call the addressee to inform him that the enclosure is missing
    C. note the omission in the margin of the letter
    D. forward the letter without taking any action

18. While opening the envelope containing official correspondence, you accidentally cut the enclosed letter.
    Of the following, the BEST action for you to take is to
    A. leave the material as it is
    B. put it together by using transparent mending tape
    C. keep it together by putting it back in the envelope
    D. keep it together by using paper clips

19. Suppose your supervisor is on the telephone in his office and an applicant arrives for a scheduled interview with him.
    Of the following, the BEST procedure to follow ordinarily is to
    A. informally chat with the applicant in your office until your supervisor has finished his phone conversation
    B. escort him directly into your supervisor's office and have him wait for him there
    C. inform your supervisor of the applicant's arrival and try to make the applicant feel comfortable while waiting
    D. have him hang up his coat and tell him to go directly in to see your supervisor

20. The length of time that files should be kept is GENERALLY
    A. considered to be seven years
    B. dependent upon how much new material has accumulated in the files
    C. directly proportionate to the number of years the office has been in operation
    D. dependent upon the type and nature of the material in the files

21. Cross-referencing a document when you file it means
    A. making a copy of the document and putting the copy into a related file
    B. indicating on the front of the document the name of the person who wrote it, the date it was written, and for what purpose
    C. putting a special sheet or card in a related file to indicate where the document is filed
    D. indicating on the document where it is to be filed

22. Unnecessary handling and recording of incoming mail could be eliminated by
    A. having the person who opens it initial it
    B. indicating on the piece of mail the names of all the individuals who should see it
    C. sending all incoming mail to more than one central location
    D. making a photocopy of each piece of incoming mail

23. Of the following, the office tasks which lend themselves MOST readily to planning and study are
    A. repetitive, occur in volume, and extend over a period of time
    B. cyclical in nature, have small volume, and extend over a short period of time
    C. tasks which occur only once in a great while not according to any schedule, and have large volume
    D. special tasks which occur only once, regardless of their volume and length of time

24. A good recordkeeping system includes all of the following procedures EXCEPT the
    A. filing of useless records
    B. destruction of certain files
    C. transferring of records from one type of file to another
    D. creation of inactive files

25. Assume that, as a supervisor, you are responsible for orienting and training new employees in your unit.
    Which of the following can MOST properly be omitted from your discussions with a new employee?
    A. The purpose of commonly used office forms
    B. Time and leave regulations
    C. Procedures for required handling of routine business calls
    D. The reason the last employee was fired

KEY (CORRECT ANSWERS)

1. A
2. D
3. B
4. B
5. A

6. C
7. C
8. C
9. B
10. C

11. A
12. B
13. D
14. D
15. C

16. D
17. C
18. B
19. C
20. D

21. C
22. B
23. A
24. A
25. D

EXAMINATION SECTION
TEST 1

DIRECTIONS: Each question or incomplete statement is followed by several suggested answers or completions. Select the one that BEST answers the question or completes the statement. *PRINT THE LETTER OF THE CORRECT ANSWER IN THE SPACE AT THE RIGHT.*

1. A multi-line telephone with buttons for eight separate lines, plus a *hold* button, is often used when an office requires more than one outside line.
   If you are talking on one line of this type of office phone when another call comes in, what is the procedure to follow if you want to answer the second call but keep the first call on the line?
   Push the
   A. *hold* button at the same time as you push the *pickup* button of the ringing line
   B. *hold* button and then push the *pickup* button of the ringing line
   C. *pickup* button of the ringing line and then push the *hold* button
   D. *pickup* button of the ringing line and push the *hold* button when you return to the original line

2. Suppose that you are asked to prepare a petty cash statement for March. The original and one copy are to go to the personnel office. One copy is to go to the fiscal office, and another copy is to go to your supervisor. The last copy is for your files.
   In preparing the statement and the copies, how many sheets of copy paper should you use?
   A. 3   B. 4   C. 5   D. 8

3. Which one of the following is the LEAST important advantage of putting the subject of a letter in the heading to the right of the address? It
   A. makes filing of the copy easier
   B. makes more space available in the body of the letter
   C. simplifies distribution of letters
   D. simplifies determination of the subject of the letter

4. Of the following, the MOST efficient way to put 100 copies of a one-page letter into 9½" x 4⅛" envelopes for mailing is to fold _____ into an envelope.
   A. each letter and insert it immediately after folding
   B. each letter separately until all 100 are folded; then insert each one
   C. the 100 letters two at a time, then separate them and insert each one
   D. two letters together, slip them apart, and insert each one

5. When preparing papers for filing, it is NOT desirable to
   A. smooth papers that are wrinkled
   B. use paper clips to keep related papers together in the files
   C. arrange the papers in the order in which they will be filed
   D. mend torn papers with cellophane tape

6. Of the following, the BEST reason for a clerical unit to have its own duplicating machine is that the unit
   A. uses many forms which it must reproduce internally
   B. must make two copies of each piece of incoming mail for a special file
   C. must make seven copies of each piece of outgoing mail
   D. must type 200 envelopes each month for distribution to the same offices

7. Several offices use the same photocopying machine.
   If each office must pay its share of the cost of running this machine, the BEST way of determining how much of this cost should be charged to each of these offices is to
   A. determine the monthly number of photocopies made by each office
   B. determine the monthly number of originals submitted for photocopying by each office
   C. determine the number of times per day each office uses the photocopying machine
   D. divide the total cost of running the photocopy machine by the total number of offices using the machine

8. Which one of the following would it be BEST to use to indicate that a file folder has been removed from the files for temporary use in another office?
   A(n)
   A. cross-reference card   B. tickler file marker
   C. aperture card   D. out guide

9. Which one of the following is the MOST important objective of filing?
   A. Giving a secretary something to do in her spare time
   B. Making it possible to locate information quickly
   C. Providing a place to store unneeded documents
   D. Keeping extra papers from accumulating on workers' desks

10. If a check has been made out for an incorrect amount, the BEST action for the writer of the check to take is to
    A. erase the original amount and enter the correct amount
    B. cross out the original amount with a single line and enter the correct amount above it
    C. black out the original amount so that it cannot be read and enter the correct amount above it
    D. write a new check

11. Which one of the following BEST describes the usual arrangement of a tickler file?
    A. Alphabetical   B. Chronological
    C. Numerical   D. Geographical

12. Which one of the following is the LEAST desirable filing practice?
    A. Using staples to keep papers together
    B. Filing all material without regard to date
    C. Keeping a record of all materials removed from the files
    D. Writing filing instructions on each paper prior to filing

13. Assume that one of your duties is to keep records of the office supplies used by your unit for the purpose of ordering new supplies when the old supplies run out.
    The information that will be of MOST help in letting you know when to reorder supplies is the
    A. quantity issued   B. quantity received
    C. quantity on hand   D. stock number

Questions 14-19.

DIRECTIONS: Questions 14 through 19 consist of sets of names and addresses. In each question, the name and address in Column II should be an exact copy of the name and address in Column I. If there is
a mistake *only* in the name, mark your answer A;
a mistake *only* in the address, mark your answer B;
a mistake in *both* name and address, mark your answer C;
no mistake in either name or address, mark your answer D.

SAMPLE QUESTION

Column I	Column II
Michael Filbert	Michael Filbert
456 Reade Street	645 Reade Street
New York, N.Y. 10013	New York, N.Y. 10013

Since there is a mistake only in the address (the street number should be 456 instead of 645), the answer to the sample question is B.

COLUMN I	COLUMN II
14. Esta Wong 141 West 68 St. New York, N.Y. 10023	Esta Wang 141 West 68 St. New York,, N.Y. 10023
15. Dr. Alberto Grosso 3475 12th Avenue Brooklyn, N.Y. 11218	Dr. Alberto Grosso 3475 12th Avenue Brooklyn, N.Y. 11218

Column I | Column II

16. Mrs. Ruth Bortlas
    482 Theresa Ct.
    Far Rockaway, N.Y. 11691

    Ms. Ruth Bortlas
    482 Theresa Ct.
    Far Rockaway, N.Y. 11169

    16._____

17. Mr. and Mrs. Howard Fox
    2301 Sedgwick Avenue
    Bronx, N.Y. 10468

    Mr. and Mrs. Howard Fox
    231 Sedgwick Ave.
    Bronx, N.Y. 10458

    17._____

18. Miss Marjorie Black
    223 East 23 Street
    New York, N.Y. 10010

    Miss Margorie Black
    223 East 23 Street
    New York, N.Y. 10010

    18._____

19. Michelle Herman
    806 Valley Rd.
    Old Tappan, N.J. 07675

    Michelle Hermann
    806 Valley Dr.
    Old Tappan, N.J. 07675

    19._____

Questions 20-25.

DIRECTIONS: Questions 20 through 25 are to be answered SOLELY on the basis of the information in the following passage.

Basic to every office is the need for proper lighting. Inadequate lighting is a familiar cause of fatigue and serves to create a somewhat dismal atmosphere in the office. One requirement of proper lighting is that it be of an appropriate intensity. Intensity is measured in foot-candles. According to the Illuminating Engineering Society of New York, for casual seeing tasks such as in reception rooms, inactive file rooms, and other service areas, it is recommended that the amount of light be 30 foot-candles. For ordinary seeing tasks such as reading and work in active file rooms and in mail rooms, the recommended lighting is 100 foot-candles. For very difficult seeing tasks such as accounting, transcribing, and business machine use, the recommended lighting is 150 foot-candles.

Lighting intensity is only one requirement. Shadows and glare are to be avoided. For example, the larger the proportion of a ceiling filled with lighting units, the more glare-free and comfortable the lighting will be. Natural lighting from windows is not too dependable because on dark wintry days, windows yield little usable light, and on sunny afternoons, the glare from windows may be very distracting. Desks should not face the windows. Finally, the main lighting source ought to be overhead and to the left of the user.

20. According to the above passage, insufficient light in the office may cause

    A. glare   B. shadows   C. tiredness   D. distraction

    20._____

21. Based on the above passage, which of the following must be considered when planning lighting arrangements?
    The
    A. amount of natural light present
    B. amount of work to be done
    C. level of difficulty of work to be done
    D. type of activity to be carried out

    21._____

22. It can be inferred from the above passage that a well-coordinated lighting scheme is LIKELY to result in
    A. greater employee productivity
    B. elimination of light reflection
    C. lower lighting cost
    D. more use of natural light
    22.____

23. Of the following, the BEST title for the above passage is
    A. Characteristics of Light
    B. Light Measurement Devices
    C. Factors to Consider When Planning Lighting Systems
    D. Comfort vs. Cost When Devising Lighting Arrangements
    23.____

24. According to the above passage, a foot-candle is a measurement of the
    A. number of bulbs used
    B. strength of the light
    C. contrast between glare and shadow
    D. proportion of the ceiling filled with lighting units
    24.____

25. According to the above passage, the number of foot-candles of light that would be needed to copy figures onto a payroll is _____ foot-candles.
    A. less than 30   B. 30   C. 100   D. 150
    25.____

KEY (CORRECT ANSWERS)

1.	B		11.	B
2.	B		12.	B
3.	B		13.	C
4.	A		14.	A
5.	B		15.	D
6.	A		16.	C
7.	A		17.	B
8.	D		18.	A
9.	B		19.	C
10.	D		20.	C

21.	D
22.	A
23.	C
24.	B
25.	D

TEST 2

DIRECTIONS: Each question or incomplete statement is followed by several suggested answers or completions. Select the one that BEST answers the question or completes the statement. *PRINT THE LETTER OF THE CORRECT ANSWER IN THE SPACE AT THE RIGHT.*

1. Assume that a supervisor has three subordinates who perform clerical tasks. One of the employees retires and is replaced by someone who is transferred from another unit in the agency. The transferred employee tells the supervisor that she has worked as a clerical employee for two years and understands clerical operations quite well. The supervisor then assigns the transferred employee to a desk, tells the employee to begin working, and returns to his own desk.
   The supervisor's action in this situation is
   A. *proper;* experienced clerical employees do not require training when they are transferred to new assignments
   B. *improper;* before the supervisor returns to his desk, he should tell the other two subordinates to watch the transferred employee perform the work
   C. *proper;* if the transferred employee makes any mistakes, she will bring them to the supervisor's attention
   D. *improper;* the supervisor should find out what clerical tasks the transferred employee has performed and give her instruction in those which are new or different

   1.____

2. Assume that you are falling behind in completing your work assignments and you believe that your workload is too heavy.
   Of the following, the BEST course of action for you to take FIRST is to
   A. discuss the problem with your supervisor
   B. decide which of your assignments can be postponed
   C. try to get some of your co-workers to help you out
   D. plan to take some of the work home with you in order to catch up

   2.____

3. Suppose that one of the clerks under your supervision is filling in monthly personnel forms. She asks you to explain a particular personnel regulation which is related to various items on the forms. You are not thoroughly familiar with the regulation.
   Of the following responses you may make, the one which will gain the MOST respect from the clerk and which is generally the MOST advisable is to
   A. tell the clerk to do the best she can and that you will check her work later
   B. inform the clerk that you are not sure of a correct explanation but suggest a procedure for her to follow
   C. give the clerk a suitable interpretation so that she will think you are familiar with all regulations
   D. tell the clerk that you will have to read the regulation more thoroughly before you can give her an explanation

   3.____

4. Charging out records until a specified due date, with prompt follow-up if they are not returned, is a
   A. *good* idea; it may prevent the records from being kept needlessly on someone's desk for long periods of time
   B. *good* idea; it will indicate the extent of your authority to other departments
   C. *poor* idea; the person borrowing the material may make an error because of the pressure put upon him to return the records
   D. *poor* idea; other departments will feel that you do not trust them with the records and they will be resentful

Questions 5-9.

DIRECTIONS: Questions 5 through 9 consist of three lines of code letters and numbers. The numbers on each line should correspond with the code letters on the same line in accordance with the table below.

Code Letter	P	L	I	J	B	O	H	U	C	G
Corresponding Letter	0	1	2	3	4	5	6	7	8	9

On some of the lines, an error exists in the coding. Compare the letters and numbers in each question carefully. If you find an error or errors on
only one of the lines in the question, mark your answer A;
any two lines in the question, mark your answer B;
all three lines in the question, mark your answer C;
none of the lines in the question, mark your answer D.

SAMPLE QUESTION
JHOILCP   3652180
BICLGUP   4286970
UCIBHLJ   5824613

In the above sample, the first line is correct since each code letter listed has the correct corresponding number. On the second line, an error exists because code letter L should have the number 1 instead of the number 6. On the third line, an error exists because the code letter U should have the number 7 instead of the number 5. Since there are errors on two of the three lines, the correct answer is B.

5. BULJCIP   4713920
   HIGPOUL   6290571
   OCUHJJBI   5876342

6. CUBLOIJ   8741023
   LCLGCLB   1818914
   JPUHIOC   3076158

7. OIJGCBPO   52398405
   UHPBLIOP   76041250
   CLUIPGPC   81720908

8. BPCOUOJI   40875732   8._____
    UOHCIPLB   75682014
    GLHUUCBJ   92677843

9. HOIOHJLH   65256361   9._____
    IOJJHHBP   25536640
    OJHBJOPI   53642502

Questions 10-13.

DIRECTIONS: Questions 10 through 13 are to be answered SOLELY on the basis of the information given in the following passage.

The mental attitude of the employee toward safety is exceedingly important in preventing accidents. All efforts designed to keep safety on the employee's mind and to keep accident prevention a live subject in the office will help substantially in a safety program. Although it may seem strange, it is common for people to be careless. Therefore, safety education is a continuous process.

Safety rules should be explained, and the reasons for their rigid enforcement should be given to employees. Telling employees to be careful or giving similar general safety warnings and slogans is probably of little value. Employees should be informed of basic safety fundamentals. This can be done through staff meetings, informal suggestions to employees, movies, and safety instruction cards. Safety instruction cards provide the employees with specific suggestions about safety and serve as a series of timely reminder helping to keep safety on the minds of employees. Pictures, posters, and cartoon sketches on bulletin boards that are located in areas continually used by employees arouse the employees' interest in safety. It is usually good to supplement this type of safety promotion with intensive individual follow-up.

10. The above passage implies that the LEAST effective of the following safety measures is   10._____
    A. rigid enforcement of safety rules
    B. getting employees to think in terms of safety
    C. elimination of unsafe conditions in the office
    D. telling employees to stay alert at all times

11. The reason given by the passage for maintaining ongoing safety education is that   11._____
    A. people are often careless
    B. office tasks are often dangerous
    C. the value of safety slogans increases with repetition
    D. safety rules change frequently

12. Which one of the following safety aids is MOST likely to be preferred by the passage? A   12._____
    A. cartoon of a man tripping over a carton and yelling, *Keep aisles clear!*
    B. poster with a large number one and a caption saying, *Safety First*

C. photograph of a very neatly arranged office
D. large sign with the word *THINK* in capital letters

13. Of the following, the BEST title for the above passage is   13.____
    A. Basic Safety Fundamentals
    B. Enforcing Safety Among Careless Employees
    C. Attitudes Toward Safety
    D. Making Employees Aware of Safety

Questions 14-21.

DIRECTIONS: Questions 14 through 21 are to be answered SOLELY on the basis of the information and chart given below.

The following chart shows expenses in five selected categories for a one-year period, expressed as percentages of these same expenses during the previous year. The chart compares two different offices. In Office T (represented by ▒▒▒▒), a cost reduction program has been tested for the past year. The other office, Office Q (represented by ////), served as a control, in that no special effort was made to reduce costs during the past year.

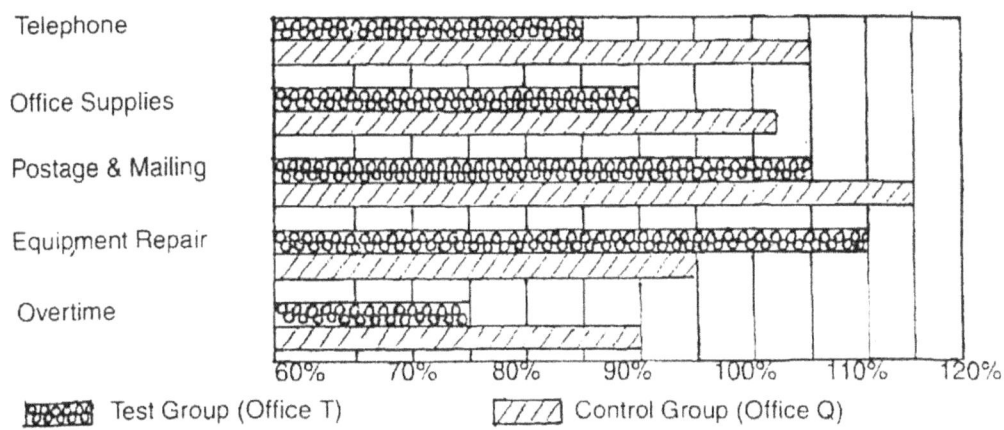

RESULTS OF OFFICE COST REDUCTION PROGRAM
Expenses of Test and Control Groups for 2020
Expressed as Percentages of Same Expenses for 2019

14. In Office T, which category of expense showed the greatest percentage   14.____
    REDUCTION from 2019 to 2020?
    A. Telephone   B. Office Supplies
    C. Postage & Mailing   D. Overtime

15. In which expense category did Office T show the BEST results in percentage   15.____
    terms when compared to Office Q?
    A. Telephone   B. Office Supplies
    C. Postage & Mailing   D. Overtime

16. According to the above chart, the cost reduction program was LEAST effective for the expense category of
    A. Office Supplies
    B. Postage & Mailing
    C. Equipment Repair
    D. Overtime

17. Office T's telephone costs went down during 2020 by approximately how many percentage points?
    A. 15
    B. 20
    C. 85
    D. 104

18. Which of the following changes occurred in expenses for Office Supplies in Office Q in the year 2020 as compared with the year 2019?
    They
    A. increased by more than 100%
    B. remained the same
    C. decreased by a few percentage points
    D. increased by a few percentage points

19. For which of the following expense categories do the results in Office T and the results in Office Q differ MOST NEARLYY by 10 percentage points?
    A. Telephone
    B. Postage & Mailing
    C. Equipment Repair
    D. Overtime

20. In which expense category did Office Q's costs show the GREATEST percentage increase in 2020?
    A. Telephone
    B. Office Supplies
    C. Postage & Mailing
    D. Equipment Repair

21. In Office T, by approximately what percentage did overtime expense change during the past year? It
    A. *increased* by 15%
    B. *increased* by 75%
    C. *decreased* by 10%
    D. *decreased* by 25%

22. In a particular agency, there were 160 accidents in 2017. Of these accidents, 75% were due to unsafe acts and the rest were due to unsafe conditions. In the following year, a special safety program was established. The number of accidents in 2019 due to unsafe acts was reduced to 35% of what it had been in 2017.
    How many accidents due to unsafe acts were there in 2019?
    A. 20
    B. 36
    C. 42
    D. 56

23. At the end of every month, the petty cash fund of Agency A is reimbursed for payments made from the fund during the month. During the month of February, the amounts paid from the fund were entered on receipts as follows: 10 bus fares of $3.50 each and one taxi fare of $35.00. At the end of the month, the money left in the fund was in the following denominations: 15 ten-dollar bills, 10 one-dollar bills, 40 quarters, and 100 dimes.
    If the petty cash fund is reduced by 20% for the following month, how much money will there be available in the petty cash fund for March?
    A. $110.00
    B. $200.00
    C. $215.00
    D. $250.00

24. The one of the following records which it would be MOST advisable to keep in alphabetical order is a
    A. continuous listing of phone messages, including time and caller, for your supervisor
    B. listing of individuals currently employed by your agency in a particular title
    C. record of purchases paid for by the petty cash fund
    D. dated record of employees who have borrowed material from the files in your office

25. Assume that you have been asked to copy by hand a column of numbers with two decimal places from one record to another. Each number consists of three, four, and five digits.
    In order to copy them quickly and accurately, you should copy
    A. each number exactly, making sure that the column of digits farthest to the right is in a straight line and all other columns are lined up
    B. the column of digits farthest to the right and then copy the next column of digits moving from right to left
    C. the column of digits farthest to the left and then copy the next column of digits moving from left to right
    D. the digits to the right of each decimal point and then copy the digits to the left of each decimal point

KEY (CORRECT ANSWERS)

1.	D		11.	A
2.	A		12.	A
3.	D		13.	D
4.	A		14.	D
5.	A		15.	A
6.	C		16.	C
7.	D		17.	A
8.	B		18.	D
9.	C		19.	B
10.	D		20.	C

21. D
22. C
23. B
24. B
25. A

EXAMINATION SECTION
TEST 1

DIRECTIONS: Each question or incomplete statement is followed by several suggested answers or completions. Select the one that BEST answers the question or completes the statement. *PRINT THE LETTER OF THE CORRECT ANSWER IN THE SPACE AT THE RIGHT.*

1. Records of one type or another are kept in every office. The MOST important of the following reasons for the supervisor of a clerical or stenographic unit to keep statistical records of the work done in his unit is generally to
   A. supply basic information needed in planning the work of the unit
   B. obtain statistics for comparison with other units
   C. serve as the basis for unsatisfactory employee evaluation
   D. provide the basis for special research projects on program budgeting

   1._____

2. It is better for an employee to report and be responsible directly to several supervisors than to report and be responsible to only one supervisor.
   This statement directly CONTRADICTS the supervisory principle generally known as
   A. span of control
   B. unity of command
   C. delegation of authority
   D. accountability

   2._____

3. The one of the following which would MOST likely lead to friction among clerks in a unit is for the unit supervisor to
   A. defend the actions of his clerks when discussing them with his own supervisor
   B. praise each of his clerks in confidence as the best clerk in the unit
   C. get his men to work together as a team in completing the work of the unit
   D. consider the point of view of the rank and file clerks when assigning unpleasant tasks

   3._____

4. You become aware that one of the employees you supervise has failed to follow correct procedure and has been permitting various reports to be prepared, typed, and transmitted improperly.
   The BEST action for you to take FIRST in this situation is to
   A. order the employee to review all departmental procedures and reprimand him for having violated them
   B. warn the employee that he must obey regulations because uniformity is essential for effective departmental operation
   C. confer with the employee both about his failure to follow regulations and his reasons for doing so
   D. watch the employee's work very closely in the future but say nothing about this violation

   4._____

5. The supervisory clerk who would be MOST likely to have poor control over his subordinates is the one who
   A. goes to unusually great lengths to try to win their approval
   B. pitches in with the work they are doing during periods of heavy workload when no extra help can be obtained
   C. encourages and helps his subordinates toward advancement
   D. considers suggestions from his subordinates before establishing new work procedures involving them

5.____

6. Suppose that a clerk who has been transferred to your office from another division in your agency because of difficulties with his supervisor has been placed under your supervision.
   The BEST course of action for you to take FIRST is to
   A. instruct the clerk in the duties he will be performing in your office and make him feel wanted in his new position
   B. analyze the clerk's past grievance to determine if the transfer was the best solution to the problem
   C. advise him of the difficulties his former supervisor had with other employees and encourage him not to feel bad about the transfer
   D. warn him that you will not tolerate any nonsense and that he will be under continuous surveillance while assigned to you

6.____

7. A certain office supervisor takes the initiative to represent his employees' interests related to working conditions, opportunities for advancement, etc. to his own supervisor and the administrative levels of the agency.
   This supervisor's actions will MOST probably have the effect of
   A. preventing employees from developing individual initiative in their work goals
   B. encouraging employees to compete openly for the special attention of their supervisor
   C. depriving employees of the opportunity to be represented by persons and/or unions of their own choosing
   D. building employee confidence in their supervisor and a spirit of cooperation in their work

7.____

8. Suppose that you have been promoted, assigned as a supervisor of a certain unit, and asked to reorganize its functions so that specific routine procedures can be established.
   Before deciding which routines to establish, the FIRST of the following steps you should take is to
   A. decide who will perform each task in the routine
   B. determine the purpose to be served by each routine procedure
   C. outline the sequence of steps in each routine to be established
   D. calculate if more staff will be needed to carry out the new procedures

8.____

9. When routine procedures covering the ordinary work of an office are established, the supervisor of the office tends to be relieved of the need to
   A. make repeated decisions on the handling of recurring similar situations
   B. check the accuracy of the work completed by his subordinates
   C. train his subordinates in new work procedures
   D. plan and schedule the work of his office

10. Of the following, the method which would be LEAST helpful to a supervisor in effectively applying the principles of on-the-job safety to the daily work of his unit is for him to
    A. initiate corrections of unsafe layouts of equipment and unsafe work processes
    B. take charge of operations that are not routine to make certain that safety precautions are established and observed
    C. continue to talk safety and promote safety consciousness in his subordinates
    D. figure the cost of all accidents which could possibly occur on the job

11. A clerk is assigned to serve as receptionist for a large and busy office. Although many members of the public visit this office, the clerk often experiences periods of time in which he has nothing to do.
    In these circumstances, the MOST advisable of the following actions for the supervisor to take is to
    A. assign a number of relatively low priority clerical jobs to the receptionist to do in the slow periods
    B. regularly rotate this assignment so that all of the clerks experience this lighter work load
    C. assign the receptionist job as part of the duties of a number of clerks whose desks are nearest the reception room
    D. overlook the situation since most of the receptionist's time is spent in performing a necessary and meaningful function

12. For a supervisor to require all stenographers in a stenographic pool to produce the same amount of work on a particular day is
    A. advisable since it will prove that the supervisor plays no favorites
    B. fair since all stenographers are receiving approximately the same salary, their output should be equivalent
    C. not necessary since the fast workers will compensate for the slow workers
    D. not realistic since individual differences in abilities and work assignment must be taken into consideration

13. The establishment of a centralized typing pool to service the various units in an organization is MOST likely to be worthwhile when there is
    A. wide fluctuation from time to time in the needs of the various units for typing service
    B. a large volume of typing work to be done in each of the units
    C. a need by each unit for different kinds of typing service
    D. a training program in operation to develop and maintain typing skills

14. A newly appointed supervisor should learn as much as possible about the backgrounds of his subordinates. This statement is GENERALLY correct because
    A. knowing their backgrounds assures they will be treated objectively, equally, and without favor
    B. effective handling of subordinates is based upon knowledge of their individual differences
    C. subordinates perform more efficiently under one supervisor than under another
    D. subordinates have confidence in a supervisor who knows all about them

15. The use of electronic computers in modern businesses has produced many changes in office and information management.
    Of the following, it would NOT be correct to state that computer utilization
    A. broadens the scope of managerial and supervisory authority
    B. establishes uniformity in the processing and reporting of information
    C. cuts costs by reducing the personnel needed for efficient office operation
    D. supplies management rapidly with up-to-date data to facilitate decision-making

16. The CHIEF advantage of having a single, large open office instead of small partitioned ones for a clerical unit or stenographic pool is that the single, large open office
    A. afford privacy without isolation for all office workers not directly dealing with the public
    B. assures the smoother, more continuous inter-office flow of work that is essential for efficient work production
    C. facilitates the office supervisor's visual control over and communication with his subordinates
    D. permits a more decorative and functional arrangement of office furniture and machines

17. When a supervisor provides a new employee with the information necessary for a basic knowledge and a general understanding of practices and procedures of the agency, he is applying the type of training generally known as _____ training.
    A. pre-employment
    B. induction
    C. on-the-job
    D. supervisory

18. Many government agencies require the approval by a central forms control unit of the design and reproduction of new office forms.
    The one of the following results of this procedure that is a DISADVANTAGE is that requiring prior approval of a central forms control unit usually
    A. limits the distribution of forms to those offices with justifiable reasons for receiving them
    B. permits checking whether existing forms or modifications of them are in line with current agency needs

C. encourages reliance on only the central office to set up all additional forms when needed
D. provides for someone with a specialized knowledge of forms design to review and criticize new and revised forms

19. Suppose that a large quantity of information is in the files which are located a good distance from your desk. Almost every worker in your office must use these files constantly. Your duties in particular require that you refer daily to about 25 of the same items. They are short, one-page items distributed throughout the files.
In this situation, your BEST course would be to
    A. take the items that you use daily from the files and keep them on your desk, inserting out cards in their place
    B. go to the files each time you need the information so that the items will be there when other workers need them
    C. make Xerox copies of the information you use most frequently and keep them in your desk for ready reference
    D. label the items you use most often with different colored tabs for immediate identification

20. Of the following, the MOST important advantage of preparing manuals of office procedures in loose-leaf form is that this form
    A. permits several employees to use different sections simultaneously
    B. facilitates the addition of new material and the removal of obsolete material
    C. is more readily arranged in alphabetical order
    D. reduces the need for cross-references to locate material carried under several headings

21. Suppose that you establish a new clerical procedure for the unit you supervise. Your keeping a close check on the time required by your staff to handle the new procedure is WISE mainly because such a check will find out
    A. whether your subordinates know how to handle the new procedure
    B. whether a revision of the unit's work schedule will be necessary as a result of the new procedure
    C. what attitude your employees have toward the new procedure
    D. what alterations in job descriptions will be necessitated by the new procedure

22. From the viewpoint of an office supervisor, the BEST of the following reasons for distributing the incoming mail before the beginning of the regular work day is that
    A. distribution can be handled quickly and most efficiently at that time
    B. distribution later in the day may be distracting to or interfere with other employees
    C. the employees who distribute the mail can then perform other tasks during the rest of the day
    D. office activities for the day based on the mail may then be started promptly

23. Suppose you are the head of a unit with ten staff members who are located in several different rooms.
If you want to inform your staff of a minor change in procedure, the BEST and LEAST expensive way of doing so would usually be to
   A. send a copy to each staff member
   B. call a special staff meeting and announce the change
   C. circulate a memo, having each staff member initial it
   D. have a clerk tell each member of the staff about the change

24. The numbered statements below relate to the stenographic skill of taking dictation. According to authorities on secretarial practices, which of these are generally recommended guides to development of efficient stenographic skills?
   I. A stenographer should date her notebook daily to facilitate locating certain notes at a later time.
   II. A stenographer should make corrections of grammatical mistakes while her boss is dictating to her.
   III. A stenographer should draw a line through the dictated matter in her notebook after she has transcribed it
   IV. A stenographer should write in longhand unfamiliar names and addresses dictated to her.

   The CORRECT answer is:
   A. Only Statements I, II, and III are generally recommended guides.
   B. Only Statements II, III, and IV are generally recommended guides.
   C. Only Statements I, III, and IV are generally recommended guides.
   D. All four statements are generally recommended guides.

25. A bureau of a city agency is about to move to a new location.
Of the following, the FIRST step that should be taken in order to provide a good layout for the office at the new location is to
   A. decide the exact amount of space to be assigned to each unit of the bureau
   B. decide whether to lay out a single large open office or one consisting of small partitioned units
   C. ask each unit chief in the bureau to examine the new location and submit a request for the amount of space he needs
   D. prepare a detailed plan of the dimensions of the floor space to be occupied by the bureau at the new location

26. Of the following, the BEST reason for discarding a sheet of carbon paper is that
   A. some carbon rubs off on your fingers when handled
   B. there are several creases in the sheet
   C. the short edge of the sheet is curled
   D. the finish on the sheet is smooth and shiny

27. Suppose you are the supervisor of a mailroom of a large city agency where the mail received daily is opened by machine, sorted by hand for delivery, and time-stamped. Letters and any enclosures are removed from envelopes and stapled together before distribution. One of your newest clerks asks you what should be done when a letter makes reference to an enclosure but no enclosure is in the envelope.
You should tell him that, in this situation, the BEST procedure is to
   A. make an entry of the sender's name and address in the missing enclosures file and forward the letter to its proper destination
   B. return the letter to its sender, attaching a request for the missing enclosure
   C. put the letter aside until a proper investigation may be made concerning the missing enclosure
   D. route the letter to the person for whom it is intended, noting the absence of the enclosure on the letter-margin

28. The term *work flow*, when used in connection with office management or the activities in an office, GENERALLY means the
   A. use of charts in the analysis of various office functions
   B. rate of speed at which work flows through a single section of an office
   C. step-by-step physical routing of work through its various procedures
   D. number of individual work units which can be produced by the average employee

29. Physical conditions can have a definite effect on the efficiency and morale of an office. Which of the following statements about physical conditions in an office is CORRECT?
   A. Hard, non-porous surfaces reflect more noise than linoleum on the top of a desk.
   B. Painting in tints of bright yellow is more appropriate for sunny, well-lit offices than for dark, poorly-lit offices.
   C. Plate glass is better than linoleum for the top of a desk.
   D. The central typing room needs less light than a conference room does.

30. In a certain filing system, documents are consecutively numbered as they are filed, a register is maintained of such consecutively numbered documents, and a record is kept of the number of each document removed from the files and its destination.
This system will NOT help in
   A. finding the present whereabouts of a particular document
   B. proving the accuracy of the data recorded on a certain document
   C. indicating whether observed existing documents were ever filed
   D. locating a desired document without knowing what its contents are

31. In deciding the kind and number of records an agency should keep, the administrative staff must recognize that records are of value in office management PRIMARILY as
    A. informational bases for agency activities
    B. data for evaluating the effectiveness of the agency
    C. raw material on which statistical analyses are to be based
    D. evidence that the agency is carrying out its duties and responsibilities

32. Complaints are often made by the public about the government's procedures. Although in most cases such procedures cannot be changed since various laws and regulations require them, it may still be possible to reduce the number of complaints.
    Which one of the following actions by personnel dealing with applicants for city services is LEAST likely to reduce complaints concerning city procedures?
    A. Treating all citizens alike and explaining to them that no exceptions to required procedures can be made.
    B. Explaining briefly to the citizen why he should comply with regulations.
    C. Being careful to avoid mistakes which may make additional interviews or correspondence necessary.
    D. Keeping the citizen informed of the progress of his correspondence when immediate disposition cannot be made.

33. Persons whose native language is not English sometimes experience difficulty in communication when visiting public offices.
    The MOST common method used by such persons to overcome the difficulty in communication is to
    A. write in their own language whatever they wish to say
    B. hire a professional interpreter
    C. ask a patrolman for assistance
    D. bring with them an English-speaking friend or relative

34. In answering a complaint made by a member of the public that a certain essential procedure required by your agency is difficult to follow, it would be BEST for you to stress most
    A. that a change in the rules may be considered if enough complaints are received
    B. why the operation of a large agency sometimes proves a hardship in individual cases
    C. the necessity for the procedure
    D. the origin of the procedure

35. When talking to a citizen, it is BEST for an employee of government to
    A. use ordinary conversational phrases and a natural manner
    B. try to copy the pronunciation and level of education shown by the citizen
    C. try to speak in a very cultured manner and tone
    D. use technical terms to show his familiarity with his own work

36. Employees who service the public should maintain an attitude which is both sympathetic and objective. An unsympathetic and subjective attitude would be shown by a public employee who
    A. says *no* with a smile when a citizen's request must be denied
    B. listens attentively to a long complaint from a citizen about government's *red tape*
    C. responds with sarcasm when a citizen asks a question which has an obvious manner
    D. suggests a definite solution to a citizen's problems

37. Of the following methods of conducting an interview, the BEST is to
    A. ask questions with *yes* or *no* answers
    B. listen carefully and ask only questions that are pertinent
    C. fire questions at the interviewee so that he must answer sincerely and briefly
    D. read standardized questions to the person being interviewed

38. An interviewer should begin with topics which are easy to talk about and which are not threatening. This procedure is useful MAINLY because it
    A. allows the applicant a little time to get accustomed to the situation and leads to freer communication
    B. distracts the attention of the person being interviewed from the main purpose of the questioning
    C. is the best way for the interviewer to show that he is relaxed and confident on the job
    D. causes the interviewee to feel that the interviewer is apportioning valuable questioning time

39. The initial interview will normally be more of a problem to the interviewer than any subsequent interviews he may have with the same person because
    A. the interviewee is likely to be hostile
    B. there is too much to be accomplished in one session
    C. he has less information about the client than he will have later
    D. some information may be forgotten when later making record of this first interview

40. You are a supervisor in an agency and are holding your first interview with a new employee. In this interview, you should strive MAINLY to
    A. show the new employee that you are an efficient and objective supervisor, with a completely impersonal attitude toward your subordinate
    B. complete the entire orientation process including the giving of detailed job-duty instructions
    C. make it clear to the employee that all your decisions are based on your many years of experience
    D. lay the groundwork for a good employee-supervisor relationship by gaining the new employee's confidence

41. Most successful interviews are those in which the interviewer shows a genuine interest in the person he is questioning. This attitude would MOST likely cause the individual being interviewed to
    A. feel that the interviewer already knows all the facts in his case
    B. act more naturally and reveal more of his true feelings
    C. request that the interviewer give more attention to his problems, not his personality
    D. react defensively, suppress his negative feelings, and conceal the real facts in his case

42. Questions worded so that the person being interviewed has some hint of the desired answer can modify the person's response. The result of the inclusion of such questions in an interview, even when they are used inadvertently, is to
    A. have no effect on the basic content of the information given by the person interviewed
    B. have value in convincing the person that the suggested plan is the best for him
    C. cause the person to give more meaningful information
    D. reduce the validity of the information obtained from the person

43. The person MOST likely to be a good interviewer is one who
    A. is able to outguess the person being interviewed
    B. tries to change the attitudes of the persons he interviews
    C. controls the interview by skillfully dominating the conversation
    D. is able to imagine himself in the position of the person being interviewed

44. The *halo effect* is an overall impression on the interviewer, whether favorable or unfavorable, usually created by a single trait. This impression then influences the appraisal of all other factors.
    A *halo effect* is LEAST likely to be created at an interview where the interviewee is a
    A. person of average appearance and ability
    B. rough-looking man who uses abusive language
    C. young attractive woman being interviewed by a man
    D. person who demonstrates an exceptional ability to remember facts

45. Of the following, the BEST way for an interviewer to calm a person who seems to have become emotionally upset as a result of a question asked is for the interviewer to
    A. talk to the person about other things for a short time
    B. ask that the person control himself
    C. probe for the cause of his emotional upset
    D. finish the questioning as quickly as possible

46. Of the following, a centralized filing system is LEAST suitable for filing
    A. material which is confidential in nature
    B. routine correspondence
    C. periodic reports of the divisions of the department
    D. material used by several divisions of the department

11 (#1)

47. Form letters should be used MAINLY when
    A. an office has to reply to a great many similar inquiries
    B. the type of correspondence varies widely
    C. it is necessary to have letters which are well-phrased and grammatically correct
    D. letters of inquiry have to be answered as soon as possible after they are received

48. Suppose that you are assigned to prepare a form from which certain information will be posted in a ledger. It would be MOST helpful to the person posting the information in the ledger is, in designing the form, you were to
    A. use the same color paper for both the form and the ledger
    B. make the form the same size as the pages of the ledger
    C. have the information on the form in the same order as that used in the ledger
    D. include in the form a box which is to be initialed when the data on the form have been posted in the ledger

49. A misplaced record is a lost record. Of the following, the MOST valid implication of this statement in regard to office work is that
    A. all records in an office should be filed in strict alphabetical order
    B. accuracy in filing is essential
    C. only one method of filing should be used throughout the office
    D. files should be locked when not in use

50. James Jones is applying for a provisional appointment as a clerk in your department. He presents a letter of recommendation from a former employer stating: *James Jones was rarely late or absent; he has a very pleasing manner and never got into an argument with his fellow employees.*
    The above information concerning this applicant
    A. proves clearly that he produces more work than the average employee
    B. indicates that he was probably attempting to conceal his inefficiency from his former employer
    C. presents no conclusive evidence of his ability to do clerical work
    D. indicates clearly that with additional training he will make a good supervisor

KEY (CORRECT ANSWERS)

1. A	11. A	21. B	31. A	41. B
2. B	12. D	22. D	32. A	42. D
3. B	13. A	23. C	33. D	43. D
4. C	14. B	24. C	34. C	44. A
5. A	15. A	25. D	35. A	45. A
6. A	16. C	26. B	36. C	46. A
7. D	17. B	27. D	37. B	47. A
8. B	18. C	28. C	38. A	48. C
9. A	19. C	29. A	39. C	49. B
10. D	20. B	30. B	40. D	50. C

TEST 2

DIRECTIONS: Each question or incomplete statement is followed by several suggested answers or completions. Select the one that BEST answers the question or completes the statement. *PRINT THE LETTER OF THE CORRECT ANSWER IN THE SPACE AT THE RIGHT.*

Questions 1-10.

DIRECTIONS: In each of Questions 1 through 10, there is a quotation which contains a word (one of those underlined) that is either incorrectly used because it is not in keeping with the meaning the quotation is evidently intended to convey, or is misspelled. There is only one incorrect word in each quotation. Of the four underlined words in each question, determine if the first one should be replaced by the word lettered A, the second replaced by the word lettered B, the third replaced by the word lettered C, or the fourth replaced by the word lettered D. Print the letter of the replacement word you have selected in the space at the right.

1. Whether one depends on flourescent or artificial light or both, adequate standards should be maintained by means of systematic tests.
   A. natural   B. safeguards   C. established   D. routine
   1._____

2. A policeman has to be prepared to assume his knowledge as a social scientist in the community.
   A. forced   B. role   C. philosopher   D. street
   2._____

3. It is practically impossible to tell whether a sentence is very long simply by measuring its length.
   A. almost   B. mark   C. too   D. denoting
   3._____

4. By using carbon paper, the typist easily is able to insert as many as six copies of a report.
   A. adding   B. seldom   C. make   D. forms
   4._____

5. Although all people have many traits in common, a receptionist in her agreements with people learns quickly how different each person is from every other person.
   A. impressions   B. associations   C. decides   D. various
   5._____

6. Strong leaders are required to organize a community for delinquency prevention and for dissemination of organized crime and drug addiction.
   A. tactics   B. important   C. control   D. meetings
   6._____

7. The demonstrators, who were taken to the Criminal Courts building in Manhattan (because it was large enough to accommodate them), contended that the arrests were unwarrented.
   A. demonstraters   B. Manhatten   C. accomodate   D. unwarranted
   7._____

8. When two or more forms for spelling a word exist, it is <u>advisable</u> to use the <u>preferred</u> spelling indicated in the <u>dictionary</u>, and to use it <u>consistantly</u>. 8._____
   A. adviseable   B. prefered   C. dictionery   D. consistently

9. If you know the language of the <u>foreign</u> country you are visiting, your <u>embarassment</u> will <u>disappear</u> and you will learn a lot more about the customs and <u>characteristics</u>. 9._____
   A. foriegn   B. embarrassment
   C. dissappear   D. charactaristics

10. Material consisting of government bulletins, <u>adverticements</u>, <u>catalogues</u>, <u>announcements</u> of address changes and any other <u>periodical</u> material of this nature, may be filed alphabetically according to subject. 10._____
    A. advertisements   B. cataloges
    C. announcments   D. pereodical

Questions 11-14.

DIRECTIONS: Each of the two sentences in Questions 11 through 14 may contain errors in punctuation, capitalization, or grammar.
If there is an error in only Sentence I, mark your answer A.
If there is an error in only Sentence II, mark you answer B.
If there is an error in both Sentences I and II, mark your answer C.
If both Sentences I and II are correct, mark your answer D.

11. I. It is very annoying to have a pencil sharpener, which is not in proper working order. 11._____
    II. The building watchman checked the door of Charlie's office and found that the lock has been jammed.

12. I. Since he went on the New York City council a year ago, one of his primary concerns has been safety in the streets. 12._____
    II. After waiting in the doorway for about 15 minutes, a black sedan appeared.

13. I. When you are studying a good textbook is important. 13._____
    II. He said he would divide the money equally between you and me.

14. I. The question is, "How can a large number of envelopes be sealed rapidly without the use of a sealing machine?" 14._____
    II. The administrator assigned two stenographers, Mary and I, to the new bureau.

Questions 15-16.

DIRECTIONS: In each of Questions 15 and 16, the four sentences are from a paragraph in a report. They are not in the right order. Which of the following arrangements is the BEST one?

15. I. An executive may answer a letter by writing his reply on the face of the letter itself instead of having a return letter typed.
    II. This procedure is efficient because it saves the executive's time, the typist's time, and saves office file space.
    III. Copying machines are used in small offices as well as large offices to save time and money in making brief replies to business letters.
    IV. A copy is made on a copying machine to go into the company files, while the original is mailed back to the sender.

    The CORRECT answer is:
    A. I, II, IV, III   B. I, IV, II, III   C. III, I, IV, II   D. III, IV, II, I

16. I. Most organizations favor one of the types but always include the others to a lesser degree.
    II. However, we can detect a definite trend toward greater uses of symbolic control.
    III. We suggest that our local police agencies are today primarily utilizing material control.
    IV. Control can be classified into three types: physical, material, and symbolic.

    The CORRECT answer is:
    A. IV, II, III, I   B. II, I, IV, III   C. III, IV, II, I   D. IV, I, III, II

17. Of the following, the MOST effective report writing style is usually characterized by
    A. covering all the main ideas in the same paragraph
    B. presenting each significant point in a new paragraph
    C. placing the least important points before the most important points
    D. giving all points equal emphasis throughout the report

18. Of the following, which factor is COMMON to all types of reports?
    A. Presentation of information
    B. Interpretation of findings
    C. Chronological ordering of the information
    D. Presentation of conclusions and recommendations

19. When writing a report, the one of the following which you should do FIRST is
    A. set up a logical work schedule
    B. determine your objectives in writing the report
    C. select your statistical material
    D. obtain the necessary data from the files

4 (#2)

20. Generally, the frequency with which reports are to be submitted or the length of the interval which they cover should depend MAINLY on the
    A. amount of time needed to prepare the reports
    B. degree of comprehensiveness required in the reports
    C. availability of the data to be included in the reports
    D. extent of the variations in the data with the passage of time

20.____

21. The objectiveness of a report is its unbiased presentation of the facts.
    If this be so, which of the following reports listed below is likely to be the MOST objective?
    A. The Best Use of an Electronic Computer in Department Z
    B. The Case for Raising the Salaries of Employees in Department A
    C. Quarterly Summary of Production in the Duplicating Unit of Department Y
    D. Recommendation to Terminate Employee X's Services Because of Misconduct

21.____

Questions 22-27.

DIRECTIONS: Questions 22 through 27 are to be answered SOLELY on the basis of the information contained in the charts below which relate to the budget allocations of City X, a small suburban community. The charts depict the annual budget allocations by Department and by Expenditures over a five-year period.

CITY X BUDGET IN MILLIONS OF DOLLARS

TABLE I. Budget Allocations By Department					
Department	2012	2013	2014	2015	2016
Public Safety	30	45	50	40	50
Health and Welfare	50	75	90	60	70
Engineering	5	8	10	5	8
Human Resources	10	12	20	10	22
Conversation and Environment	10	15	20	20	15
Education and Development	15	25	35	15	15
TOTAL BUDGET	120	180	225	150	180

TABLE II. Budget Allocations by Expenditures					
Category	2012	2013	2014	2015	2016
Raw Materials and Machinery	36	63	68	30	98
Capital Outlay	12	27	56	15	18
Personal Services	72	90	101	105	65
TOTAL BUDGET	120	180	225	150	180

22. The year in which the SMALLEST percentage of the total annual budget was allocated to the Department of Education and Development is
    A. 2012   B. 2013   C. 2015   D. 2016

22.____

23. Assume that, in 2015, the Department of Conservation and Environment divided its annual budget into the three categories of expenditures and in exactly the same proportion as the budget shown in Table II for the year 2015. The amount allocated for capital outlay in the Department of Conservation and Environment's 2015 budget was MOST NEARLY _____ million.
    A. $2
    B. $4
    C. $6
    D. $10

24. From the year 2013 to the year 2015, the sum of the annual budgets for the Departments of Public Safety and Engineering showed an overall _____ of _____ million.
    A. decline; $8
    B. increase; $7
    C. decline; $15
    D. increase; $22

25. The LARGEST dollar increase in departmental budget allocations from one year to the next was in
    A. Public Safety from 2012 to 2013
    B. Health and Welfare from 2012 to 2013
    C. Education and Development from 2014 to 2015
    D. Human Resources from 2014 to 2015

26. During the five-year period, the annual budget of the Department of Human Resources was GREATER than the annual budget for the Department of Conservation and Environment in _____ of the years.
    A. none
    B. one
    C. two
    D. three

27. If the total City X budget increases at the same rate from 2016 to 2017 as it did from 2015 to 2016, the total City X budget for 2017 will be MOST NEARLY _____ million.
    A. $180
    B. $200
    C. $210
    D. $215

Questions 28-34.

DIRECTIONS: Questions 28 through 34 are to be answered SOLELY on the basis of the information contained in the graph below which relates to the work of a public agency.

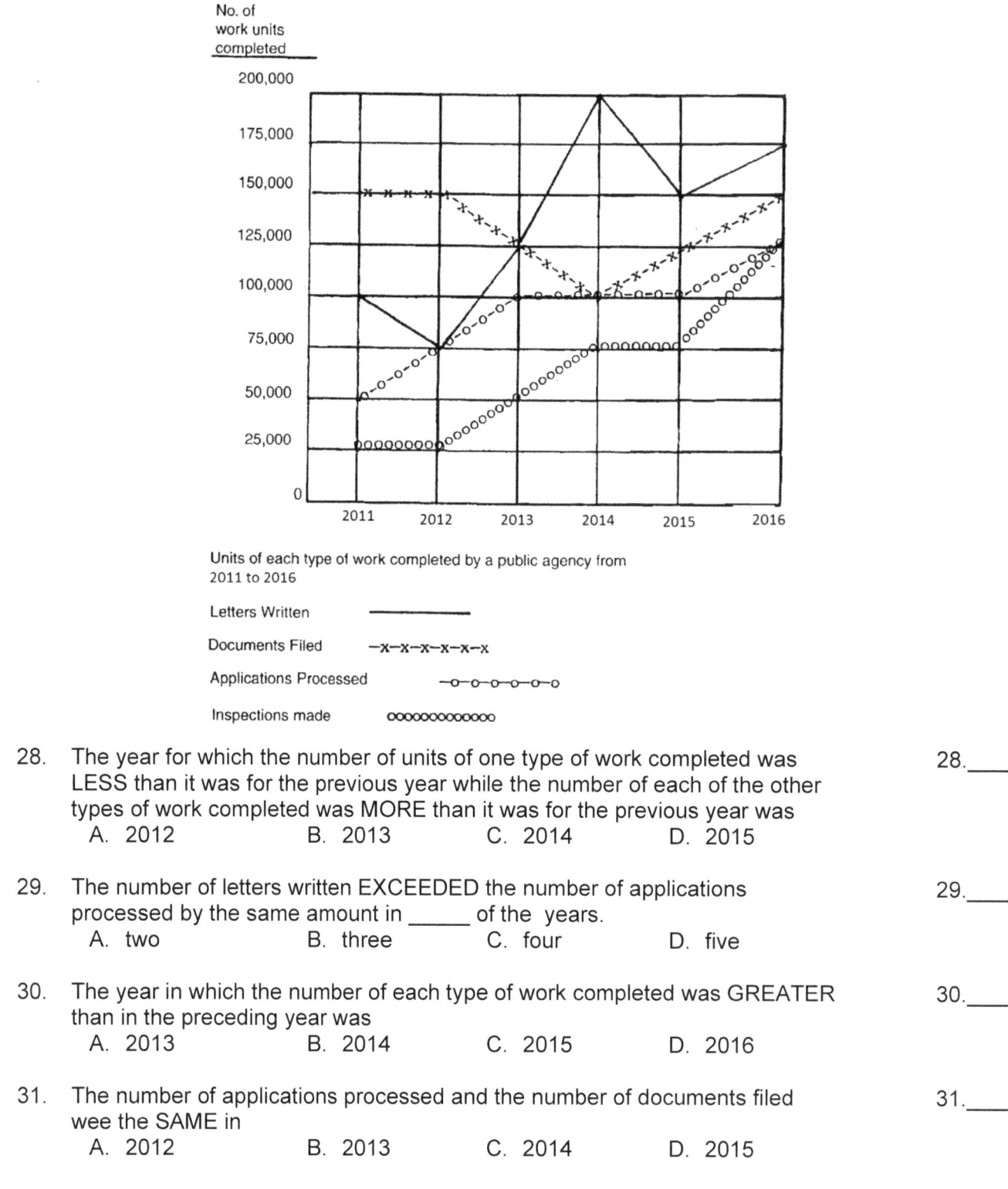

Units of each type of work completed by a public agency from 2011 to 2016

Letters Written ─────────
Documents Filed ─x─x─x─x─x─x
Applications Processed ─o─o─o─o─o─o
Inspections made ooooooooooooo

28. The year for which the number of units of one type of work completed was LESS than it was for the previous year while the number of each of the other types of work completed was MORE than it was for the previous year was
 A. 2012 B. 2013 C. 2014 D. 2015

28.____

29. The number of letters written EXCEEDED the number of applications processed by the same amount in _____ of the years.
 A. two B. three C. four D. five

29.____

30. The year in which the number of each type of work completed was GREATER than in the preceding year was
 A. 2013 B. 2014 C. 2015 D. 2016

30.____

31. The number of applications processed and the number of documents filed wee the SAME in
 A. 2012 B. 2013 C. 2014 D. 2015

31.____

32. The TOTAL number of units of work completed by the agency 32._____
    A. increased in each year after 2011
    B. decreased from the prior year in two of the years after 2011
    C. was the same in two successive years from 2011 to 2016
    D. was less in 2011 than in any of the following years

33. For the year in which the number of letters written was twice as high as it 33._____
    was in 2011, the number of documents filed was _____ it was in 2011.
    A. the same as   B. two-thirds of what
    C. five-sixths of what   D. 1½ times what

34. The variable which was the MOST stable during the period 2011 through 34._____
    2016 was
    A. Inspections Made   B. Letters Written
    C. Documents Filed   D. Applications Processed

Questions 35-41.

DIRECTIONS: Questions 35 through 41 are to be answered SOLELY on the basis of the information in the following passage.

Job evaluation and job rating systems are intended to introduce scientific procedures. Any type of approach, when properly used, will give satisfactory results. The Point System, when properly validated by actual use, is more likely to be suitable for general use than the ranking system. In many aspects, the Factor Comparison Plan is a point system tied to money values. Of course, there may be another system that combines the ranking system with the point system, especially during the initial stages of the development of the program. After the program has been in use for some time, the tendency is to drop off the ranking phrase and continue the use of the point system.

In the ranking system of rating of jobs, every job within the plant is arranged in some order, either from the one with the simplest qualifications to the one with maximum requirements, or in the reverse order. This system should be preceded by careful job analysis and the writing of accurate job descriptions before the rating process is undertaken. It is possible, of course, to take the jobs as they are found in the business enterprise and use the names as they are without any attempt at standardization, and merely rank them according to the general overall impression of the raters. Such a procedure is certain to fall short of what may reasonably be expected of job rating. Another procedure that is in reality merely a modification of the simple rating described above is to establish a series of grades or zones and arrange all the jobs in the plant into groups within these grades and zones. The practice in most common use is to arrange all the jobs in the plant according to their requirements by rating them and then to establish the classifications or groups.

The actual ranking of jobs may be done by one individual, several individuals, or a committee. If several individuals are working independently on the task, it will usually be found that, in general, they agree but that their rankings vary in certain details. A conference between the individuals, with each person giving his reasons why he rated one way or another, usually produces agreement. The detailed job descriptions are particularly helpful when there is disagreement among raters as to the rating of certain jobs. It is not only possible but desirable to have workers participate in the construction of the job description and in rating the job.

8 (#2)

35. The MAIN theme of this passage is
    A. the elimination of bias in job rating
    B. the rating of jobs by the ranking system
    C. the need for accuracy in allocating points in the point system
    D. pitfalls to avoid in selecting key jobs in the Factor Comparison Plan

36. The ranking system of rating jobs consists MAINLY of
    A. attaching a point value to each ratable factor of each job prior to establishing an equitable pay scale
    B. arranging every job in the organization in descending order and then following this up with a job analysis of the key jobs
    C. preparing accurate job descriptions after a job analysis and then arranging all jobs either in ascending or descending order based on job requirements
    D. arbitrarily establishing a hierarchy of job classes and grades and then fitting each job into a specific class and grade based on the opinions of unit supervisors

37. The above passage states that the system of classifying jobs MOST used in an organization is to
    A. organize all jobs in the organization in accordance with their requirements and then create categories or clusters of jobs
    B. classify all jobs in the organization according to the titles and ranks by which they are currently known in the organization
    C. establish a pre-arranged series of grades or zones and then fit all jobs into one of the grades or zones
    D. determine the salary currently being paid for each job, and then rank the jobs in order according to salary

38. According to the above passage, experience has shown that when a group of raters is assigned to the job evaluation task and each individual rates independently of the others, the raters GENERALLY
    A. *agree* with respect to all aspects of their rankings
    B. *disagree* with respect to all or nearly all aspects of the rankings
    C. *disagree* on overall ratings but agree on specific rating factors
    D. *agree* on overall rankings but have some variance in some details

39. The above passage states that the use of a detailed job description is of SPECIAL value when
    A. employees of an organization have participated in the preliminary steps involved in actual preparation of the job description
    B. labor representatives are not participating in ranking of the jobs
    C. an individual rater who is unsure of himself is ranking the jobs
    D. a group of raters is having difficulty reaching unanimity with respect to ranking a certain job

35. ____
36. ____
37. ____
38. ____
39. ____

40. A comparison of the various rating systems as described in the above passage shows that
    A. the ranking system is not as appropriate for general use as a properly validated point system
    B. the point system is the same as the Factor Comparison Plan except that it places greater emphasis on money
    C. no system is capable of combining the point system and the Factor Comparison Plan
    D. the point system will be discontinued last when used in combination with the Factor Comparison System

41. The above passage implies that the PRINCIPAL reason for creating job evaluation and rating systems was to help
    A. overcome union opposition to existing salary plans
    B. base wage determination on a more objective and orderly foundation
    C. eliminate personal bias on the part of the trained scientific job evaluators
    D. management determine if it was overpricing the various jobs in the organizational hierarchy

42. As a general rule, in a large office it is desirable to have more than one one employee who is able to operate any one machine and more than one office machine capable of performing any one type of required operation. According to this statement, there USUALLY should be
    A. fewer office machines in an office than are necessary for efficient job performance
    B. more office machines in an office than there are employees able to operate them
    C. more types of required operations to be performed than there are machines necessary to their performance
    D. fewer types of required operations to be performed than there are machines capable of performing them

43. The plan of an organization's structure and procedures may appear to be perfectly sound, but the organization may still operate wastefully and with a great amount of friction because of the failure of the people in the organization to work together.
    The MOST valid implication of this statement is that
    A. inefficiency within an organization may be caused by people being directed to do the wrong things
    B. an organization which operates inefficiently might be improved by revising its systems and methods of operations
    C. use of the best methods an organization can devise may not prevent an organization from being inefficient
    D. the people in an organization may not have an appreciation of the high quality of the organization's plan of operations

44. If an employee is to be held responsible for obtaining results, he should be given every reasonable freedom to exercise his own intelligence and initiative to achieve the results expected.
The MOST valid implication of this statement is that
   A. the authority delegated should match the responsibility assigned
   B. achieving results depends upon the individual's willingness to work
   C. the most important aspect of getting a job done is to know how to do it
   D. understanding the requirements of a task is essential to its accomplishment

45. Essentially, an organization is defined as any group of individuals who are cooperating under the direction of executive leadership in an attempt to accomplish certain common objectives.
The one of the following which this statement does NOT include as an essential characteristic of an organization is _____ the members of the group.
   A. cooperation among
   B. proficiency of
   C. authoritative guidance of
   D. goals common to

46. A supervisor, in organizing the work activities of the staff of an office, should recognize that one of the conditions which is expected to promote a high level of interest on the part of an office worker in his job is to assign him to perform a variety of work.
The MOST valid implication of this statement is that
   A. each worker should be taught to perform each type of work in the office
   B. workers should be assigned to perform types of work in which they have expressed interest
   C. a worker who is assigned to perform a single type of work is likely to become bored
   D. some workers are likely to perform several types of work better than other workers are able to

47. Of the following basic guides to effective letter writing, which one would NOT be recommended as a way of improving the quality of business letters?
   A. Use emphatic phrases like *close proximity* and *first and foremost* to round out sentences.
   B. Break up complicated sentences by making short sentences out of dependent clauses.
   C. Replace old-fashioned phrases like *enclosed please find* and *recent date* with a more direct approach.
   D. Personalize letters by using your reader's name at least once in the body of the message.

48. Suppose that you must write a reply letter to a citizen's request for a certain pamphlet printed by your agency. The pamphlet is temporarily unavailable but a new supply will be arriving by December 8 or 9.
Of the following four sentences, which one expresses the MOST positive business letter writing approach?
   A. We cannot send the materials you requested until after December 8.
   B. May we assure you that the materials you requested will be sent as quickly as possible.
   C. We will be sending the materials you requested as soon as our supply is replenished.
   D. We will mail the materials you requested on or shortly after December 8.

49. Using form letters in business correspondence is LEAST effective when
   A. answering letters on a frequently recurring subject
   B. giving the same information to many addresses
   C. the recipient is only interested in the routine information contained in the form letter
   D. a replay must be keyed to the individual requirements of the intended reader

50. The ability to write memos and letters is very important in clerical and administrative work. Methodical planning of a reply letter usually involves the following basic steps which are arranged in random order:
   I. Determine the purpose of the letter you are about to write.
   II. Make an outline of what information your reply letter should contain.
   III. Read carefully the letter to be answered to find out its main points.
   IV. Assemble the facts to be included in your reply letter.
   V. Visualize your intended reader and adapt your letter writing style to him.
   If the above-numbered steps were arranged in their proper logical order, the one which would be THIRD in the sequence is
   A. II B. III C. IV D. V

KEY (CORRECT ANSWERS)

1. A	11. C	21. C	31. C	41. B
2. B	12. C	22. D	32. C	42. D
3. C	13. A	23. A	33. B	43. C
4. C	14. B	24. A	34. D	44. A
5. B	15. C	25. B	35. B	45. B
6. C	16. D	26. B	36. C	46. C
7. D	17. B	27. D	37. A	47. A
8. D	18. A	28. B	38. D	48. D
9. B	19. B	29. B	39. D	49. D
10. A	20. D	30. D	40. A	50. A

EXAMINATION SECTION
TEST 1

DIRECTIONS: Each question or incomplete statement is followed by several suggested answers or completions. Select the one that BEST answers the question or completes the statement. *PRINT THE LETTER OF THE CORRECT ANSWER IN THE SPACE AT THE RIGHT.*

1. One of the things that can ruin morale in a work group is the failure to exercise judgment in the assignment of overtime work to your subordinates.
   Of the following, the MOST desirable supervisory practice in assigning overtime work is to
   A. rotate overtime on a uniform basis among all your subordinates
   B. assign overtime to those who are *moonlighting* after regular work hours
   C. rotate overtime as much as possible among employees willing to work additional hours
   D. assign overtime to those employees who take frequent long weekend vacations

1.____

2. The consistent delegation of authority by you to experienced and reliable subordinates in your work group is generally considered
   A. *undesirable*, because your authority in the group may be threatened by an unscrupulous subordinate
   B. *undesirable*, because it demonstrates that you cannot handle your own workload
   C. *desirable*, because it shows that you believe that you have been accepted by your subordinates
   D. *desirable*, because the development of subordinates creates opportunities for assuming broader responsibilities yourself

2.____

3. The MOST effective way for you to deal with a false rumor circulating among your subordinates is to
   A. have a trusted subordinate state a counter-rumor
   B. recommend disciplinary action against the rumor mongers
   C. point out to your subordinates that rumors degrade both listener and initiator
   D. furnish your subordinates with sufficient authentic information

3.____

4. Two of your subordinates tell you about a mistake they made in a report that has already been sent the top management.
   Which of the following questions is most likely to elicit the MOST valuable information from your subordinates?
   A. Who is responsible?
   B. How can we explain this to top management?
   C. How did it happen?
   D. Why weren't you more careful?

4.____

5. Assume that you are responsible for implementing major changes in work flow patterns and personnel assignments in the unit of which you are in charge. The one of the following actions which is MOST likely to secure the willing cooperation of those persons who will have to change their assignments?
   A. having the top administrators of the agency urge their cooperation at a group meeting
   B. issuing very detailed and carefully planned instructions to the affected employees regarding the changes
   C. integrating employee participation into the planning of the changes
   D. reminding the affected employees that career advancement depends upon compliance with organizational objectives

6. Of the following, the BEST reason for using face-to-face communication instead of written communication is that face-to-face communication
   A. allows for immediate feedback
   B. is more credible
   C. enables greater use of detail and illustration
   D. is more polite

7. Of the following, the MOST likely disadvantage of giving detailed instructions when assigning a task to a subordinate is that such instructions may
   A. conflict with the subordinate's ideas of how the task should be done
   B. reduce standardization of work performance
   C. cause confusion in the mind of the subordinate
   D. inhibit the development of new procedures by the subordinate

8. Assume that you are a supervisor of a unit consisting of a number of subordinates and that one subordinate, whose work is otherwise acceptable, keeps on making errors in one particular task assigned to him in rotation. This task consists of routine duties which all your subordinates should be able to perform.
   Of the following, the BEST way for you to handle this situation is to
   A. do the task yourself when the erring employee is scheduled to perform it and assign this employee other duties
   B. reorganize work assignments so that the task in question is no longer performed in rotation but assigned full-time to your most capable subordinate
   C. find out why this subordinate keeps on making the errors in question and see that he learns how to do the task properly
   D. maintain a well-documented record of such errors and, when the evidence is overwhelming, recommend appropriate disciplinary action

9. In the past, Mr. T, one of your subordinates, had been generally withdrawn and suspicious of others, but he had produced acceptable work. However, Mr. T has lately started to get into arguments with his fellow workers during which he displays intense rage. Friction between this subordinate and the others in your unit is mounting and the unit's work is suffering.

Of the following, which would be the BEST way for you to handle this situation?
- A. Rearrange work schedules and assignments so as to give Mr. T no cause for complaint
- B. Instruct the other workers to avoid Mr. T and not to respond to any abuse
- C. Hold a unit meeting and appeal for harmony and submergence of individual differences in the interest of work
- D. Maintain a record of incidents and explore with Mr. T the possibility of seeking professional help

10. You are responsible for seeing to it that your unit is functioning properly in the accomplishment of its budgeted goals.
Which of the following will provide the LEAST information on how well you are accomplishing such goals?
    - A. Measurement of employee performance
    - B. Identification of alternative goals
    - C. Detection of employee errors
    - D. Preparation of unit reports

11. Some employees see an agency training program as a threat.
Of the following, the MOST likely reason for such an employee attitude toward training is that the employee involved feel that
    - A. some trainers are incompetent
    - B. training rarely solves real work-a-day problems
    - C. training may attempt to change comfortable behavior patterns
    - D. training sessions are boring

12. Of the following, the CHIEF characteristic which distinguishes a good supervisor from a poor supervisor is the good supervisor's
    - A. ability to favorably impress others
    - B. unwillingness to accept monotony or routine
    - C. ability to deal constructively with problem situations
    - D. strong drive to overcome opposition

13. Of the following, the MAIN disadvantage of on-the-job training is that, generally,
    - A. special equipment may be needed
    - B. production may be slowed down
    - C. the instructor must maintain an individual relationship with the trainee
    - D. the on-the-job instructor must be better qualified than the classroom instructor

14. All of the following are correct methods for a supervisor to use in connection with employee discipline EXCEPT
    - A. trying not to be too lenient or too harsh
    - B. informing employees of the rules and the penalties for violations of the rules
    - C. imposing discipline immediately after the violation is discovered
    - D. making sure, when you apply discipline, that the employee understands that you do not want to do it

15. Of the following, the MAIN reason for a supervisor to establish standard procedures for his unit is to
    A. increase the motivation for his subordinates
    B. make it easier for the subordinates to submit to authority
    C. reduce the number of times that his subordinates have to consult him
    D. reduce the number of mistakes that his subordinates will make

16. Of the following, the BEST reason for using form letters in correspondence is that they are
    A. concise and businesslike
    B. impersonal in tone
    C. uniform in appearance
    D. economical for large mailings

17. The use of loose-leaf office manuals for the guidance of employees on office policy, organization, and office procedures has won wide acceptance.
    The MAIN advantage of the loose-leaf format is that it
    A. allows speedy reference
    B. facilitates revisions and changes
    C. includes a complete index
    D. presents a professional appearance

18. Office forms sometimes consist of several copies, each of a different color. The MAIN reason for using different colors is to
    A. make a favorable impression on the users of the form
    B. distinguish each copy from the others
    C. facilitate the appearance of legible carbon copies
    D. reduce cost, since using colored stock permits recycling of paper

19. Which of the following is the BEST justification for obtaining a photocopying machine for the office?
    A. A photocopying machine can produce an unlimited number of copies at a low fixed cost per copy.
    B. Employees need little training in operating a photocopying machine.
    C. Office costs will be reduced and efficiency increased.
    D. The legibility of a photocopy generally is superior to copy produced by any other office duplicating device.

20. Which one of the following should be the MOST important overall consideration when preparing a recommendation to automate a large-scale office activity?
    The
    A. number of models of automated equipment available
    B. benefits and costs of automation
    C. fears and resistance of affected employees
    D. experience of offices which have automated similar activities

21. A tickler file is MOST appropriate for filing materials
    A. chronologically according to date they were received
    B. alphabetically by name
    C. alphabetically by subject
    D. chronologically according to date they should be followed up

22. Which of the following is the BEST reason for decentralizing rather than centralizing the use of duplicating machines?
    A. Developing and retaining efficient duplicating machine operators
    B. Facilitating supervision of duplicating services
    C. Motivating employees to produce legible duplicated copies
    D. Placing the duplicating machines where they are most convenient and most frequently used

23. Window envelopes are sometimes considered preferable to individually addressed envelopes PRIMARILY because
    A. window envelopes are available in standard sizes for all purposes
    B. window envelopes are more attractive and official-looking
    C. the use of window envelopes eliminates the risk of inserting a letter in the wrong envelope
    D. the use of window envelopes requires neater typing

24. In planning the layout of a new office, the utilization of space and the arrangement of staff, furnishings and equipment should usually be MOST influenced by the
    A. gross square footage
    B. status differences in the chain of command
    C. framework of informal relationships among employees
    D. activities to be performed

25. When delegating responsibility for an assignment to a subordinate, it is MOST important that you
    A. retain all authority necessary to complete the assignment
    B. make yourself generally available for consultation with the subordinate
    C. inform your superiors that you are no longer responsible for the assignment
    D. decrease the number of subordinates whom you have to supervise

KEY (CORRECT ANSWERS)

1.	C	11.	C
2.	D	12.	C
3.	D	13.	B
4.	D	14.	D
5.	C	15.	C
6.	A	16.	D
7.	D	17.	B
8.	C	18.	B
9.	D	19.	C
10.	B	20.	B

21.	D
22.	D
23.	C
24.	D
25.	B

TEST 2

DIRECTIONS: Each question or incomplete statement is followed by several suggested answers or completions. Select the one that BEST answers the question or completes the statement. *PRINT THE LETTER OF THE CORRECT ANSWER IN THE SPACE AT THE RIGHT.*

Questions 1-5.

DIRECTIONS: Questions 1 through 5 are to be answered on the basis of the following passage.

The most effective control mechanism to prevent gross incompetence on the part of public employees is a good personnel program. The personnel officer in the line departments and the central personnel agency should exert positive leadership to raise levels of performance. Although the key factor is the quality of the personnel recruited, staff members other than personnel officers can make important contributions to efficiency. Administrative analysts, now employed in many agencies, make detailed studies of organization and procedures, with the purpose of eliminating delays, waste, and other inefficiencies. Efficiency is, however, more than a question of good organization and procedures; it is also the product of the attitudes and values of the public employees. Personal motivation can provide the will to be efficient. The best management studies will not result in substantial improvement of the performance of those employees who feel no great urge to work up to their abilities.

1. The passage indicates that the key factor in preventing gross incompetence of public employees is the
   A. hiring of administrative analysts to assist personnel people
   B. utilization of effective management studies
   C. overlapping of responsibility
   D. quality of the employees hired

1.____

2. According to the above passage, the central personnel agency staff should
   A. work more closely with administrative analysts in the line departments than with personnel officers
   B. make a serious effort to avoid jurisdictional conflicts with personnel officers in line departments
   C. contribute to improving the quality of work of public employees
   D. engage in a comprehensive program to change the public's negative image of public employees

2.____

3. The passage indicates that efficiency in an organization can BEST be brought about by
   A. eliminating ineffective control mechanisms
   B. instituting sound organizational procedures
   C. promoting competent personnel
   D. recruiting people with desire to do good work

3.____

4. According to the passage, the purpose of administrative analysis in a public agency is to
   A. prevent injustice to the public employee
   B. promote the efficiency of the agency
   C. protect the interests of the public
   D. ensure the observance of procedural due process

5. The passage implies that a considerable rise in the quality of work of public employees can be brought about by
   A. encouraging positive employee attitudes toward work
   B. controlling personnel officers who exceed their powers
   C. creating warm personal associations among public employees in an agency
   D. closing loopholes in personnel organization and procedures

6. Typist X can type 20 forms per hour and Typist I can type 30 forms per hour. If there are 30 forms to be typed and both typists are put to work on the job, how soon should they be expected to finish the work? _____ minutes.
   A. 32   B. 34   C. 36   D. 38

7. Assume that there were 18 working days in February and that the six clerks in your unit had the following number of absences:
   Clerk F – 3 absences
   Clerk G – 2 absences
   Clerk H – 8 absences
   Clerk I – 1 absence
   Clerk J – 0 absences
   Clerk K – 5 absences
   The average percentage attendance for the six clerks in your unit in February was MOST NEARLY
   A. 80%   B. 82%   C. 84%   D. 86%

8. A certain employee is paid at the rate of $15.00 per hour, with time-and-a-half for overtime. Hours in excess of 40 hours a week count as overtime. During the past week, the employee put in 48 working hours.
   The employee's gross wages for the week are MOST NEARLY
   A. $600   B. $700   C. $720   D. $840

9. You are making a report on the number of inside and outside calls handled by a particular switchboard. Over a 15-day period, the total number of all inside and outside calls handled by the switchboard was 5,760. The average number of inside calls per day was 234. You cannot find one day's tally of outside calls, but the total number of outside calls for the other fourteen days was 2,065. From this information, how many outside calls must have been reported on the missing tally?
   A. 175   B. 185   C. 195   D. 205

10. A floor plan has been prepared for a new building, drawn to a scale of ¾ inch = 1 foot. A certain area is drawn 1 and ½ feet long and 6 inches wide on the floor plan.
What are the ACTUAL dimensions of this area in the new building?
_____ feet long and _____ feet wide.

    A. 21; 8   B. 24; 8   C. 27; 9   D. 30; 9

10.____

Questions 11-15.

DIRECTIONS: In answering Questions 11 through 15, assume that you are in charge of public information for an office which issues reports and answers questions from other offices and from the public on changes in land use. The following charts represent comparative land use in four neighborhoods. The area of each neighborhood is expressed in city blocks. Assume that all city blocks are the same size.

NEIGHBORHOOD A – 16 CITY BLOCKS   NEIGHBORHOOD B – 24 CITY BLOCKS

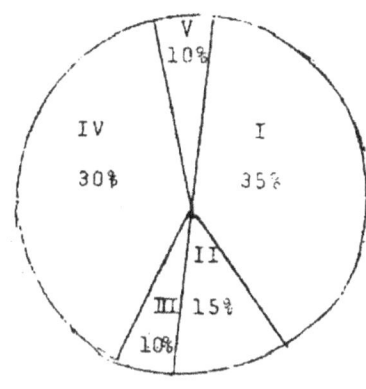 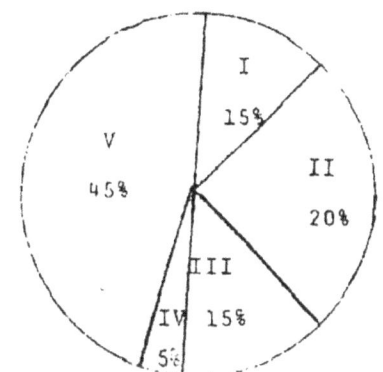

NEIGHBORHOOD C – 20 CITY BLOCKS   NEIGHBORHOOD D – 12 CITY BLOCKS

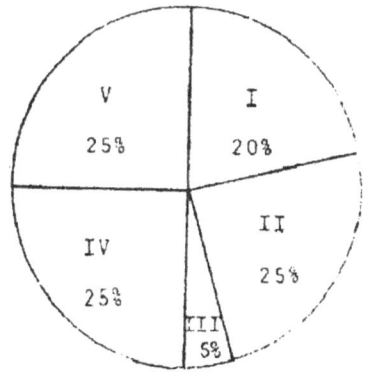 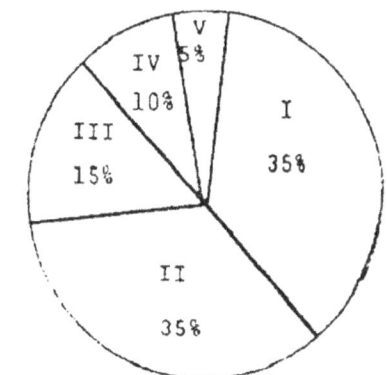

KEY: I: One- and two-family houses
        II: Apartment buildings
        III: Office buildings
        IV: Rental Stores
        V: Factories and warehouses

11. In how many of these neighborhoods does residential use (Categories I and II together) account for at least 50% of the land use?
    A. One   B. Two   C. Three   D. Four

12. Which neighborhood has the largest land area occupied by apartment buildings? Neighborhood
    A. A   B. B   C. C   D. D

13. In which neighborhood is the largest percentage of the land devoted to both office buildings and retail stores? Neighborhood _____.
    A. A   B. B   C. C   D. D

14. What is the difference, to the nearest city block, between the amount of land devoted to retail stores in Neighborhood B and the amount devoted to similar use in Neighborhood C? _____ block(s).

15. Which one of the following types of buildings occupies the same amount of land area in Neighborhood B as the amount of land area occupied by retail stores in Neighborhood A?
    A. 1   B. 2   C. 4   D. 6

Questions 16-20.

DIRECTIONS: Questions 16 through 20 are to be answered on the basis of the following passage.

For a period of nearly fifteen years, beginning in the mid-1960's, higher education sustained a phenomenal rate of growth. The factors principally responsible were continuing improvement in the rate of college entrance by high school graduates, a 50-percent increase in the size of the college-age (eighteen to twenty-one) group, and—until about 1977—a rapid expansion of university research activity supported by the federal government.

Today, as one looks ahead to the year 2030, it is apparent that each of these favorable stimuli will either be abated or turn into a negative factor. The rate of growth of the college-age group has already diminished, and from 2020 to 2025 the size of the college-age group will shrink annually almost as fast as it grew from 1975 to 1980. From 2025 to 2030, this annual decrease will slow down so that by 2030 the age-group will be about the same size as it was in 2029. This substantial net decrease in the size of the college-age group over the next fifteen years will dramatically affect college enrollments since, currently, 83 percent of undergraduates are twenty-one and under, and another 11 percent are twenty-one to twenty-four.

16. Which one of the following factors is NOT mentioned in the above passage as contributing to the high rate of growth of higher education?
    A. A larger increase in the size of the eighteen to twenty-one age group
    B. The equalization of educational opportunities among socio-economic groups
    C. The federal budget impact on research and development spending in the higher education sector
    D. The increasing rate at which high school graduates enter college

17. Based on the information in the above passage, the size of the college-age group in 2030 will be
    A. larger than it was in 2029
    B. larger than it was in 2015
    C. smaller than it was in 2025
    D. about the same as it was in 2020

18. According to the above passage, the tremendous rate of growth of higher education started around
    A. 1960   B. 1965   C. 1970   D. 1975

19. The percentage of undergraduates who are over age 24 is MOST NEARLY
    A. 6%   B. 8%   C. 11%   D. 17%

20. Which one of the following conclusions can be substantiated by the information given in the above passage?
    A. The college-age group will be about the same size in 2020 as it was in 1975.
    B. The annual decrease in the size of the college-age group from 2020 to 2025 will be about the same as the annual increase from 1975 to 1980.
    C. The overall decrease in the size of the college-age group from 2020 to 2025 will be followed by an overall increase in its size from 2025 to 2030.
    D. The size of the college-age group will decrease at a fairly constant rate from 2005 to 2020.

21. Because higher status is important to many employees, they will often make an effort to achieve it as an end in itself.
    Of the following, the BEST course of action for the supervisor to take on the basis of the preceding statement is to
    A. attach higher status to that behavior of subordinates which is directed toward reaching the goals of the organization
    B. avoid showing sympathy toward subordinates' wishes for increased wages, improved working conditions, or other benefits
    C. foster interpersonal competitiveness among subordinates so that personal friendliness is replaced by the desire to protect individual status
    D. reprimand subordinates whenever their work is in some way unsatisfactory in order to adjust their status accordingly

22. Assume that a large office in a certain organization operates long hours and is thus on two shifts with a slight overlap. Those employees, including supervisors, who are most productive are given their choice of shifts. The earlier shift is considered preferable by most employees.
    As a result of this method of assignment, which of the following is MOST likely to result?
    A. Most non-supervisory employees will be assigned to the late shift; most supervisors will be assigned to the early shift.
    B. Most supervisors will be assigned to the late shift; most non-supervisory employees will be assigned to the early shift.
    C. The early shift will be more productive than the late shift.
    D. The late shift will be more productive than the early shift.

23. Assume that a supervisor of a unit in which the employees are of average friendliness tells a newly-hired employee on her first day that her co-workers are very friendly. The other employees hear his remarks to the new employee. Which of the following is the MOST likely result of this action of the supervisor? The
    A. newly-hired employee will tend to feel less friendly than if the supervisor had said nothing
    B. newly-hired employee will tend to believe that her co-workers are very friendly
    C. other employees will tend to feel less friendly toward one another
    D. other employees will tend to see the newly-hired employee as insincerely friendly

24. A recent study of employee absenteeism showed that, although unscheduled absence for part of a week is relatively high for young employees, unscheduled absence for a full week is low. However, although full-week unscheduled absence is least frequent for the youngest employees, the frequency of such absence increases as the age of employees increases.
    Which of the following statements is the MOST logical explanation for the greater full-week absenteeism among older employees?
    A. Older employees are more likely to be males.
    B. Older employees are more likely to have more relatively serious illnesses.
    C. Younger employees are more likely to take longer vacations.
    D. Younger employees are more likely to be newly-hired.

25. An employee can be motivated to fulfill his needs as he sees them. He is not motivated by what others think he ought to have, but what he himself wants. Which of the following statements follows MOST logically from the foregoing viewpoint?
    A. A person's different traits may be separately classified, but they are all part of one system comprising a whole person.
    B. Every job, however simple, entitles the person who does it to proper respect and recognition of his unique aspirations and abilities.
    C. No matter what equipment and facilities an organization has, they cannot be put to use except by people who have been motivated.
    D. To an observer, a person's need may be unrealistic but they ae still controlling.

KEY (CORRECT ANSWERS)

1.	D	11.	B
2.	C	12.	C
3.	D	13.	A
4.	B	14.	C
5.	A	15.	D
6.	C	16.	B
7.	B	17.	C
8.	D	18.	B
9.	B	19.	A
10.	B	20.	B

21. A
22. C
23. B
24. B
25. D

EXAMINATION SECTION
TEST 1

DIRECTIONS: Each question or incomplete statement is followed by several suggested answers or completions. Select the one that BEST answers the question or completes the statement. *PRINT THE LETTER OF THE CORRECT ANSWER IN THE SPACE AT THE RIGHT.*

1. Suppose that you are requested to transmit to the stenographers in your bureau an order curtailing certain privileges that they have been enjoying. You anticipate that your staff may resent curtailment of such privileges. Of the following, the BEST action for you to take is to

    A. impress upon your staff that an order is an order and must be obeyed
    B. attempt to explain to your staff the probable reasons for curtailing their privileges
    C. excuse the curtailment of privileges by saying that the welfare of the staff was evidently not considered
    D. warn your staff that violation of an order may be considered sufficient cause for immediate dismissal

1.____

2. The supervisor should set a good example.
Of the following, the CHIEF implication of the above statement is that the supervisor should

    A. behave as he expects his workers to behave
    B. know as much about the work as his workers do
    C. keep his workers informed of what he is doing
    D. keep ahead of his workers

2.____

3. Of the following, the LEAST desirable procedure for the competent supervisor to follow is to

    A. organize his work before taking responsibility for helping others with theirs
    B. avoid schedules and routines when he is busy
    C. be flexible in planning and carrying out his responsibilities
    D. secure the support of his staff in organizing the total job of the unit

3.____

4. Evaluation helps the worker by increasing his security.
Of the following, the BEST justification for this statement is that

    A. security and growth depend upon knowledge by the worker of the agency's evaluation
    B. knowledge of his evaluation by agency and supervisor will stimulate the worker to better performance
    C. evaluation enables the supervisor and worker to determine the reasons for the worker's strengths and weaknesses
    D. the supervisor and worker together can usually recognize and deal with any worker's insecurity

4.____

5. A supervisor may encourage his subordinates to make suggestions by

    A. keeping a record of the number of suggestions an employee makes
    B. providing a suggestion box

5.____

C. outlining a list of possible suggestions
D. giving credit to a subordinate whose suggestion has been accepted and used

6. If you were required to give service ratings to employees under your supervision, you should consider as MOST important during the current period the

   A. personal characteristics and salary and grade of an employee
   B. length of service and the volume of work performed
   C. previous service rating given him
   D. personal characteristics and the quality of work of an employee

7. A supervisor must consider many factors in evaluating a worker whom he has supervised for a considerable time. In evaluating the capacity of such a worker to use independent judgment, the one of the following to which the supervisor should generally give MOST consideration is the worker's

   A. capacity to establish good relationships with people (clients and colleagues)
   B. educational background
   C. emotional stability
   D. the quality and judgment shown by the investigator in previous work situations known to the supervisor

8. Experts in the field of personnel relations feel that it is generally a bad practice for subordinate employees to become aware of pending or contemplated changes in policy or organizational set-up via the "grapevine" CHIEFLY because

   A. evidence that one or more responsible officials have proved untrustworthy will undermine confidence in the agency
   B. the information disseminated by this method is seldom entirely accurate and generally spreads needless unrest among the subordinate staff
   C. the subordinate staff may conclude that the administration feels the staff cannot be trusted with the true information
   D. the subordinate staff may conclude that the administration lacks the courage to make an unpopular announcement through official channels

9. Assume that a supervisor praises his subordinates for satisfactory aspects of their work only when he is about to criticize them for unsatisfactory aspects of their work. Such a practice is UNDESIRABLE primarily because

   A. his subordinates may expect to be praised for their work even if it is unsatisfactory
   B. praising his subordinates for some aspects of their work while criticizing other aspects will weaken the effects of the criticisms
   C. his subordinates would be more receptive to criticism if it were followed by praise
   D. his subordinates may come to disregard praise and wait for criticism to be given

10. The one of the following which would be the BEST reason for an agency to eliminate a procedure for obtaining and recording certain information is that

    A. it is no longer legally required to obtain the information
    B. there is an advantage in obtaining the information
    C. the information could be compiled on the basis of other information available
    D. the information obtained is sometimes incorrect

11. In determining the type and number of records to be kept in an agency, it is important to recognize that records are of value PRIMARILY as

    A. raw material to be used in statistical analysis
    B. sources of information about the agency's activities
    C. by-products of the activities carried on by the agency
    D. data for evaluating the effectiveness of the agency

11.____

12. Assume that you are a supervisor. One of the workers under your supervision is careless about the routine aspects of his work.
    Of the following, the action MOST likely to develop in this worker a better attitude toward job routines is to demonstrate that

    A. it is just as easy to do his job the right way
    B. organization of his job will leave more time for field work
    C. the routine part of the job is essential to performing a good piece of work
    D. job routines are a responsibility of the worker

12.____

13. A supervisor can MOST effectively secure necessary improvement in a worker's office work by

    A. encouraging the worker to keep abreast of his work
    B. relating the routine part of his job to the total job to be done
    C. helping the worker to establish a good system for covering his office work and holding him to it
    D. informing the worker that he will be required to organize his work more efficiently

13.____

14. A supervisor should offer criticism in such a manner that the criticism is helpful and not overwhelming.
    Of the following, the LEAST valid inference that can be drawn on the basis of the above statement is that a supervisor should

    A. demonstrate that the criticism is partial and not total
    B. give criticism in such a way that it does not undermine the worker's self-confidence
    C. keep his relationships with the worker objective
    D. keep criticism directed towards general work performance

14.____

15. The one of the following areas in which a worker may LEAST reasonably expect direct assistance from the supervisor is in

    A. building up rapport with all clients
    B. gaining insight into the unmet needs of clients
    C. developing an understanding of community resources
    D. interpreting agency policies and procedures

15.____

16. You are informed that a worker under your supervision has submitted a letter complaining of unfair service rating. Of the following, the MOST valid assumption for you to make concerning this worker is that he should be

    A. more adequately supervised in the future
    B. called in for a supervisory conference
    C. given a transfer to some other unit where he may be more happy
    D. given no more consideration than any other inefficient worker

16.____

17. Assume that you are a supervisor. You find that a somewhat bewildered worker, newly appointed to the department, hesitates to ask questions for fear of showing his ignorance and jeopardizing his position.
Of the following, the BEST procedure for you to follow is to

   A. try to discover the reason for his evident fear of authority
   B. tell him that when he is in doubt about a procedure or a policy he should consult his fellow workers
   C. develop with the worker a plan for more frequent supervisory conferences
   D. explain why each staff member is eager to give him available information that will help him do a good job

18. In order to teach an employee to develop an objective approach, the BEST action for the supervisor to take is to help the worker to

   A. develop a sincere interest in his job
   B. understand the varied responsibilities that are an integral part of his job
   C. differentiate clearly between himself as a friend and as an employee
   D. find satisfaction in his work

19. Of the following, the MOST effective method of helping a newly appointed employee adjust to his new job is to

   A. assure him that with experience his uncertain attitudes will be replaced by a professional approach
   B. help him, by accepting him as he is, to have confidence in his ability to handle the job
   C. help him to be on guard against the development of punitive attitudes
   D. help him to recognize the mutability of the agency's policies and procedures

20. Suppose that, as a supervisor, you have scheduled an individual conference with an experienced employee under your supervision.
Of the following, the BEST plan of action for this conference is to

   A. discuss the work that the employee is most interested in
   B. plan with the employee to cover any problems that are difficult for him
   C. advise the employee that the conference is his to do with as he sees fit
   D. spot check the employee's work in advance and select those areas for discussion in which the employee has done poor work

21. Of the following, the CHIEF function of a supervisor should be to

   A. assist in the planning of new policies and the evaluation of existing ones
   B. promote congenial relationships among members of the staff
   C. achieve optimum functioning of each unit and each worker
   D. promote the smooth functioning of job routines

22. The competent supervisor must realize the importance of planning.
Of the following, the aspect of planning which is LEAST appropriately considered a responsibility of the supervisor is

   A. long-range planning for the proper functioning of his unit
   B. planning to take care of peak and slack periods
   C. planning to cover agency policies in group conferences

D. long-range planning to develop community resources

23. The one of the following objectives which should be of LEAST concern to the supervisor in the performance of his duties is to 23.____

    A. help the worker to make friends with all of his fellow employees
    B. be impartial and fair to all members of the staff
    C. stimulate the worker's growth on the job
    D. meet the needs of the individual employee

24. The one of the following which is LEAST properly considered a direct responsibility of the supervisor is 24.____

    A. liaison between the staff and the administrator
    B. interpreting administrative orders and procedures to the employee
    C. training new employees
    D. maintaining staff morale at a high level

25. If an employee shows excessive submission which indicates a need for dependence on the supervisor in handling an assignment, it would be MOST advisable for the supervisor to 25.____

    A. indicate firmly that the employee-supervisor relationship does not call for submission
    B. define areas of responsibility of employee and of superior
    C. recognize the employee's need to be sustained and supported and help him by making decisions for him
    D. encourage the employee to do his best to overcome his handicap

KEY (CORRECT ANSWERS)

1.	B	11.	B
2.	A	12.	D
3.	B	13.	B
4.	C	14.	D
5.	D	15.	A
6.	D	16.	B
7.	D	17.	C
8.	B	18.	C
9.	D	19.	B
10.	C	20.	B

21. C
22. D
23. A
24. A
25. B

TEST 2

DIRECTIONS: Each question or incomplete statement is followed by several suggested answers or completions. Select the one that BEST answers the question or completes the statement. *PRINT THE LETTER OF THE CORRECT ANSWER IN THE SPACE AT THE RIGHT.*

1. Assume that, as a supervisor, you are conducting a group conference. 1.____
Of the following, the BEST procedure for you to follow in order to stimulate group discussion is to

    A. permit the active participation of all members
    B. direct the discussion to an acceptable conclusion
    C. resolve conflicts of opinion among members of the group
    D. present a question for discussion on which the group members have some knowledge or experience

2. Suppose that, as a new supervisor, you wish to inform the staff under your supervision of 2.____
your methods of operation. Of the following, the BEST procedure for you to follow is to

    A. advise the staff that they will learn gradually from experience
    B. inform each employee in an individual conference
    C. call a group conference for this purpose
    D. distribute a written memorandum among all members of the staff

3. The MOST constructive and effective method of correcting an employee who has made a 3.____
mistake is, in general, to

    A. explain that his evaluation is related to his errors
    B. point out immediately where he erred and tell him how it should have been done
    C. show him how to readjust his methods so as to avoid similar errors in the future
    D. try to discover by an indirect method why the error was made

4. The MOST effective method for the supervisor to follow in order to obtain the cooperation 4.____
of an employee under his supervision is, wherever possible, to

    A. maintain a careful record of performance in order to keep the employee on his toes
    B. give the employee recognition in order to promote greater effort and give him more satisfaction in his work
    C. try to gain the employee's cooperation for the good of the service
    D. advise the employee that his advancement on the job depends on his cooperation

5. Of the following, the MOST appropriate initial course for an employee to take when he is 5.____
unable to clarify a policy with his supervisor is to

    A. bring up the problem at the next group conference
    B. discuss the policy immediately with his fellow employees
    C. accept the supervisor's interpretation as final
    D. determine what responsibility he has for putting the policy into effect

6. Good administration allows for different treatment of different workers. 6.____
Of the following, the CHIEF implication of this quotation is that

A. it would be unfair for the supervisor not to treat all staff members alike
B. fear of favoritism tends to undermine staff morale
C. best results are obtained by individualization within the limits of fair treatment
D. difficult problems call for a different kind of approach

7. The MOST effective and appropriate method of building efficiency and morale in a group of employees is, in general,

   A. by stressing the economic motive
   B. through use of the authority inherent in the position
   C. by a friendly approach to all
   D. by a discipline that is fair but strict

8. Of the following, the LEAST valid basis for the assignment of work to an employee is the

   A. kind of service to be rendered
   B. experience and training of the employee
   C. health and capacity of the employee
   D. racial composition of the community where the office is located

9. The CHIEF justification for staff education, consisting of in-service training, lies in its contribution to

   A. improvement in the quality of work performed
   B. recruitment of a better type of employee
   C. employee morale accruing from a feeling of growth on the job
   D. the satisfaction that the employee gets on his job

10. Suppose that you are a supervisor. An employee no longer with your department requests you, as his former supervisor, to write a letter recommending him for a position with a private organization.
    Of the following, the BEST procedure for you to follow is to include in the letter only information that

    A. will help the applicant get the job
    B. is clear, factual, and substantiated
    C. is known to you personally
    D. can readily be corroborated by personal interview

11. Of the following, the MOST important item on which to base the efficiency evaluation of an employee under your supervision is

    A. the nature of the relationship that he has built up with his fellow employees
    B. how he gets along with his supervisors
    C. his personal habits and skills
    D. the effectiveness of his control over his work

12. According to generally accepted personnel practice, the MOST effective method of building morale in a new employee is to

    A. exercise caution in praising the employee, lest he become overconfident
    B. give sincere and frank commendation whenever possible, in order to stimulate interest and effort

C. praise the employee highly even for mediocre performance so that he will be stimulated to do better
D. warn the employee frequently that he cannot hope to succeed unless he puts forth his best effort

13. Errors made by newly appointed employees often follow a predictable pattern. The one of the following errors likely to have LEAST serious consequences is the tendency of a new employee to

    A. discuss problems that are outside his province with the client
    B. persuade the client to accept the worker's solution of a problem
    C. be too strict in carrying out departmental policy and procedure
    D. depend upon the use of authority due to his inexperience and lack of skill in working with people

14. The MOST effective way for a supervisor to break down a worker's defensive stand against supervisory guidance is to

    A. come to an understanding with him on the mutual responsibilities involved in the job of the employee and supervisor
    B. tell him he must feel free to express his opinions and to discuss basic problems
    C. show him how to develop toward greater objectivity, sensitivity, and understanding
    D. advise him that it is necessary to carry out agency policy and procedures in order to do a good job

15. Of the following, the LEAST essential function of the supervisor who is conducting a group conference should be to

    A. keep attention focused on the purpose of the conference
    B. encourage discussion of controversial points
    C. make certain that all possible viewpoints are discussed
    D. be thoroughly prepared in advance

16. When conducting a group conference, the supervisor should be LEAST concerned with

    A. providing an opportunity for the free interchange of ideas
    B. imparting knowledge and understanding of case work
    C. leading the discussion toward a planned goal
    D. pointing out where individual workers have erred in work practice

17. If the participants in a group conference are unable to agree on the proper application of a concept to the work of a department, the MOST suitable temporary procedure for the supervisor to follow is to

    A. suggest that each member think the subject through before the next meeting
    B. tell the group to examine their differences for possible conflicts with present policies
    C. suggest that practices can be changed because of new conditions
    D. state the acceptable practice in the agency and whether deviations from such practice can be permitted

18. If an employee is to participate constructively in any group discussion, it is MOST important that he have

    A. advance notice of the agenda for the meeting
    B. long experience in the department
    C. knowledge and experience in the particular work
    D. the ability to assume a leadership role

18.____

19. Of the following, the MOST important principle for the supervisor to follow when conducting a group discussion is that he should

    A. move the discussion toward acceptance by the group of a particular point of view
    B. express his ideas clearly and succinctly
    C. lead the group to accept the authority inherent in his position
    D. contribute to the discussion from his knowledge and experience

19.____

20. The one of the following which is considered LEAST important as a purpose of the group conference is to

    A. provide for a free exchange of ideas among the members of the group
    B. evaluate work methods and procedures in order to protect the members from individual criticism
    C. provide an opportunity to interpret procedures and work practices
    D. pool the experience of the group members for the benefit of all

20.____

21. In order for the evaluation conference to stimulate MOST effectively the employee's professional growth on the job, it should

    A. start him thinking, about his present status with the department
    B. show him the necessity for taking stock of his total performance
    C. give him a sense of direction in relation to his future development
    D. give him a better perspective on the work in his department

21.____

22. The development of good public relations in the area for which the supervisor is responsible should be considered by the supervisor as

    A. not his responsibility as he is primarily responsible for his employees' services
    B. dependent upon him as he is in the best position to interpret the department to the community
    C. not important to the adequate functioning of the department
    D. a part of his method of carrying out his job responsibility, as what his employees do affect the community

22.____

23. Of the following, the MOST valuable and desirable trait in a supervisor is a(n)

    A. ability to get the best work out of his men
    B. ability to inspire his men with the desire to "get ahead in the world"
    C. persuasive manner of speech
    D. tall and commanding appearance

23.____

24. The supervisor who is MOST suitable for the general practical needs of a department is the one who gets

    A. a great deal of satisfactory work done although usually handicapped by constant bickering among fellow employees
    B. a great deal of satisfactory work done because of his ability to do a large amount of it himself
    C. less work done than the other supervisors but has unusually high quality work production standards
    D. more than an average amount of satisfactory work done because of the cooperative way in which the employees work for him

25. A supervisor has been transferred to a new section.
    The BEST way for him to get cooperation from his employees would be to

    A. ask the (general manager)(chief) to give him strong support
    B. explain his policy firmly so that the employees cannot blame him for any mistakes made
    C. note the troublemakers and have them transferred out
    D. show his men that he not only is interested in getting work done but also has their welfare in mind

KEY (CORRECT ANSWERS)

1.	D	11.	D
2.	C	12.	B
3.	C	13.	C
4.	B	14.	A
5.	D	15.	B
6.	C	16.	D
7.	D	17.	D
8.	D	18.	A
9.	A	19.	D
10.	B	20.	B

21. C
22. D
23. A
24. D
25. D

TEST 3

DIRECTIONS: Each question or incomplete statement is followed by several suggested answers or completions. Select the one that BEST answers the question or completes the statement. *PRINT THE LETTER OF THE CORRECT ANSWER IN THE SPACE AT THE RIGHT.*

1. Jones and Smith, who work together, do slightly more than an average amount of work for two men together. But you find that Jones does most of the work while Smith does less than he should.
   To correct this situation, the BEST thing for you as supervisor to do would be to

   A. assign work to Smith for which he must be personally responsible
   B. make a complaint to the bureau chief about Smith but praise Jones
   C. point out to Jones that he does most of the work and that he should urge Smith to do more
   D. require Smith to do more whenever the work of both men together falls below the expected average

   1.____

2. You have given a new employee detailed instructions on how he should do a job. When you return a little later, you find that the employee was afraid to start the job because he did not completely understand your instructions.
   In this situation, it would be BEST for you to

   A. assign the man to a job where less intelligence is needed
   B. explain again, illustrating if possible how the job is to be done
   C. explain again and recommend him for dropping at the end of probation if he does not understand
   D. make the man explain why he did not at least start the job

   2.____

3. An employee does very good work but has trouble getting to work on time.
   To get him to come on time, the supervisor should

   A. bring him up on charges to stop the lateness once and for all
   B. have him report to the general manager every time he is late
   C. talk over the problem with him to find its cause and possible solution
   D. threaten to transfer him if he cannot get to work early

   3.____

4. As supervisor, you observe that an employee keeps making mistakes.
   Of the following, the BEST thing for you to do would be to

   A. make no mention of these mistakes as they gradually disappear with experience
   B. point the mistakes out to the employee in front of the other employees so all may learn from them
   C. talk to the employee privately about these mistakes and show her how to avoid them
   D. try to transfer this employee out in exchange for an employee who can do the work

   4.____

5. Proper action by the supervisor could MOST probably prevent work delays in his section caused by

   A. a large number of employees quitting their jobs in the department
   B. the daily assignments of the employees not being properly planned

   5.____

C. the inexperience of new employees transferred into his section
D. unexpected delays in processing

6. If, after careful thought, you have definitely decided that one of your employees should be disciplined, it is MOST important for you to realize that

   A. discipline is the best tool for leading workers
   B. discipline should be severe in order to get the best results
   C. the discipline should be delayed so that its full force can be felt
   D. the employee should know why she is being disciplined

7. A knowledge of the experience and abilities of the men working under him is MOST useful to a supervisor in

   A. deciding what type of discipline to exercise when necessary
   B. finding the cause of minor errors in the assignments
   C. making proper work assignments
   D. making vacation schedules

8. A supervisor will be able to train his employees better if he is familiar with basic principles of learning.
   Which one of the following statements about the learning process is MOST correct?

   A. An employee who learns one job quickly will learn any other job quickly.
   B. Emphasizing correct things done by the employee usually gives him an incentive to improve.
   C. Great importance placed on an employee's mistakes is the best way to help him to get rid of them.
   D. It is very hard to teach new methods to middle-aged or older employees.

9. Several experienced employees have resigned. You have decided to arrange for permanent transfers of other experienced employees in your section to fill their jobs, leaving only jobs that new inexperienced employees can fill easily.
   For you, the supervisor, to talk this over with the employees who will be affected by the move would be

   A. *bad;* it would show weakness and wavering by you
   B. *bad;* transfers should be made on the basis of efficiency
   C. *good;* it will help you get better cooperation from the employees involved
   D. *good;* transfers should be made on the basis of seniority

10. An employee under your supervision does much less work than he is capable of.
    What should be your FIRST step in an effort to improve his performance?

    A. Discovering why he is not working up to his full capacity
    B. Going over his mistakes and shortcomings with him to reduce them
    C. Pointing out to him that the quality of his work is below standard
    D. Showing him that the other men produce much more than he does

11. The FIRST thing a supervisor does when he assigns an employee to a new job is to find out what the employee already knows about the job.
    This practice is

A. *good;* mainly because the employees may know more than the supervisor about the job
B. *good;* mainly because this information will help the supervisor in instructing the employee
C. *poor;* mainly because since it is a new job, the employee cannot be expected to know anything
D. *poor;* mainly because the supervisor should first find out how the employee will feel toward the job

12. Your superior has assigned to you a task which, in your opinion, should not be performed at this stage of the operation.
    In this situation, it would be BEST for you to

    A. carry out the assignment since your superior is responsible
    B. refuse to carry out the assignment
    C. talk it over with the employees under you to see if they think as you do
    D. talk the matter over with your superior right away

13. It is important for a supervisor to take prompt action upon requests from subordinates MAINLY because

    A. delays in making decisions mean that they must then be made on the basis of facts which can no longer be up-to-date
    B. favorable action on such requests is more likely to result when a decision is made quickly
    C. it is an indication that the supervisor has his work well-organized
    D. promptness in such matters helps maintain good employee morale

14. As a supervisor, you realize that your superior, when under pressure, has a habit of giving you oral orders which are not always clear and also lack sufficient detail. The BEST procedure for you to follow in such situations would be to

    A. obtain clarification by requesting needed details at the time you receive such orders
    B. consider past orders of a similar nature to determine the probable intent of your superior
    C. frequently consult your superior during the course of the job in order to secure the required details to complete the job
    D. request your superior to put all his orders to you in writing

15. Some supervisors have their subordinates meet with them in group discussion of troublesome problems.
    The MAIN advantage of such group discussions as a supervisory tool is that they can be directed toward the

    A. appraisal of the personalities involved
    B. development of new policies and regulations
    C. circulation of new material and information
    D. pooling of experience in the solution of common problems

16. The PRINCIPAL disadvantage of using form letters to reply to written complaints made by the public is that such form letters

A. tend to make any investigation of the original complaint rather superficial
B. are limited by their design to handle only a few possible situations that could give rise to complaints
C. lack the desirable element of the personal touch for the recipient
D. tend to lose their effectiveness by quickly becoming obsolete

17. With respect to standard employee grievance procedure, it would be MOST correct to state that   17._____

    A. the Commissioner of Labor is the highest ranking official, excepting the judge, who can be involved in a particular grievance
    B. the person with the grievance has the right to be represented by virtually anyone he chooses
    C. the one having the grievance (the grievant) can be represented by the majority organization only if he is a member thereof
    D. time limits are not set concerning adjudication in order to insure the fullest consideration of the particular grievance

18. In order for a supervisor to employ the system of democratic leadership in his supervision, it would generally be BEST for him to   18._____

    A. allow his subordinates to assist in deciding on methods of work performance and job assignments but only in those areas where decisions have not been made on higher administrative levels
    B. allow his subordinates to decide how to do the required work, interposing his authority when work is not completed on schedule or is improperly completed
    C. attempt to make assignments of work to individuals only of the type which they enjoy doing
    D. maintain control over the job assignments and work production but allow the subordinates to select methods of work and internal conditions of work at democratically conducted staff conferences

19. In an office in which supervision has been considered quite effective, it has become necessary to press for above-normal production for a limited period to achieve a required goal.   19._____
    The one of the following which is a LEAST likely result of this pressure is that

    A. there will be more "gripings" by employees
    B. some workers will do both more and better work than has been normal for them
    C. there will be an enhanced feeling of group unity
    D. there will be increased absenteeism

20. It is the practice of some supervisors, when they believe that it would be desirable for a subordinate to take a particular action in a case, to inform the subordinate of this in the form of a suggestion rather than in the form of a direct order. In general, this method of getting a subordinate to take the desired action is   20._____

    A. *inadvisable;* it may create in the mind of the subordinate the impression that the supervisor is uncertain about the efficacy of his plan and is trying to avoid whatever responsibility he may have in resolving the case
    B. *advisable;* it provides the subordinate with the maximum opportunity to use his own judgment in handling the case

C. *inadvisable;* it provides the subordinate with no clear-cut direction and, therefore, is likely to leave him with a feeling of uncertainty and frustration
D. *advisable;* it presents the supervisor's view in a manner which will be most likely to evoke the subordinate's cooperation

21. At a group training conference conducted by a supervisor, one of the employees asks a question which is only partially related to the subject under discussion. He believes that the question was asked to embarrass him since he recently reprimanded the employees for inattention to his work. Under these circumstances, it would generally be BEST for the assistant supervisor to

    A. pointedly ignore the question and the questioner and go on to other matters
    B. request the questioner to remain after the group session, at which time the question and the questioner's attitude will be considered
    C. state that he does not know the answer and ask for a volunteer to give a brief answer, brief because the question is only partially relevant
    D. tell the questioner that the question is not pertinent, show wherein it is not pertinent, and state that the time of the group should not be wasted on it

22. The one of the following circumstances when it would generally be MOST proper for a supervisor to do a job himself rather than to train a subordinate to do the job is when it is

    A. a job which the supervisor enjoys doing and does well
    B. not a very time-consuming job but an important one
    C. difficult to train another to do the job yet is not difficult for the supervisor to do
    D. unlikely that this or any similar job will have to be done again at any future time

23. Effective training of subordinates requires that the supervisor understand certain facts about learning and forgetting processes.
    Among these is the fact that people generally

    A. both learn and forget at a relatively constant rate and this rate is dependent upon their general intellectual capacity
    B. forget what they learned at a much greater rate during the first day than during subsequent periods
    C. learn at a relatively constant rate except for periods of assimilation when the quantity of retained learning decreases while information is becoming firmly fixed in the mind
    D. learn very slowly at first when introduced to a new topic, after which there is a great increase in the rate of learning

24. It has been suggested that a subordinate who likes his supervisor will tend to do better work than one who does not. According to the MOST widely-held current theories of supervision, this suggestion is a

    A. *bad one;* since personal relationships tend to interfere with proper professional relationships
    B. *bad one;* since the strongest motivating factors are fear and uncertainty
    C. *good one;* since liking one's supervisor is a motivating factor for good work performance
    D. *good one;* since liking one's supervisor is the most important factor in employee performance

25. A supervisor is supervising an employee who is very soon to complete his six months' probationary period. The supervisor finds him to be slow, to make many errors, to do work poorly, to be antagonistic toward the supervisor, and to be disliked by most of his co-workers. The supervisor is aware that he is the sole support of his wife and two children. He has never been late or absent during his service with the department. If he is terminated, there will be a considerable delay before a replacement for him arrives.
It would generally be BEST for the supervisor to recommend that this employee be

   A. transferred to work with another supervisor and other staff members with whom he may get along better
   B. retained but be very closely supervised until his work shows marked improvement
   C. retained since his services are needed with the expectation that he be terminated at some later date when a replacement is readily available
   D. terminated

KEY (CORRECT ANSWERS)

1.	A	11.	B
2.	B	12.	D
3.	C	13.	D
4.	C	14.	A
5.	B	15.	D
6.	D	16.	C
7.	C	17.	B
8.	B	18.	A
9.	C	19.	D
10.	A	20.	D

21. C
22. D
23. B
24. C
25. D

READING COMPREHENSION
UNDERSTANDING AND INTERPRETING WRITTEN MATERIAL

EXAMINATION SECTION

TEST 1

DIRECTIONS: Each question or incomplete statement is followed by several suggested answers or completions. Select the one that BEST answers the question or completes the statement. *PRINT THE LETTER OF THE CORRECT ANSWER IN THE SPACE AT THE RIGHT.*

Questions 1-3.

DIRECTIONS: Questions 1 through 3 are to be answered SOLELY on the basis of the following passage.

Every organization needs a systematic method of checking its operations as a means to increase efficiency and promote economy. Many successful private firms have instituted a system of audit or internal inspections to accomplish these ends. Law enforcement organizations, which have an extremely important service to *sell*, should be no less zealous in developing efficiency and economy in their operations. Periodic, organized, and systematic inspections are one means of promoting the achievement of these objectives. The necessity of an organized inspection system is perhaps greatest in those law enforcement groups which have grown to such a size that the principal officer can no longer personally supervise or be cognizant of every action taken. Smooth and effective operation demands that the head of the organization have at hand some tool with which he can study and enforce general policies and procedure and also direct compliance with day-to-day orders, most of which are put into execution outside his sight and hearing. A good inspection system can serve as that tool.

1. The central thought of the above passage is that a system of inspections within a police department
    A. is unnecessary for a department in which the principal officer can personally supervise all official actions taken
    B. should be instituted at the first indication that there is any deterioration in job performance by the force
    C. should be decentralized and administered by first-line supervisory officers
    D. is an important aid to the police administrator in the accomplishment of law enforcement objectives

2. The MOST accurate of the following statements concerning the need for an organized inspection system in a law enforcement organization is: It is
    A. never needed in an organization of small size where the principal officer can give personal supervision
    B. most needed where the size of the organization prevents direct supervision by the principal officer
    C. more needed in law enforcement organizations than in private firms
    D. especially needed in an organization about to embark upon a needed expansion of services

3. According to the above passage, the head of the police organization utilizes the internal inspection system
   A. as a tool which must be constantly re-examined in the light of changing demands for police service
   B. as an administrative technique to increase efficiency and promote economy
   C. by personally visiting those areas of police operation which are outside his sight and hearing
   D. to augment the control of local commanders over detailed field operations

3._____

Questions 4-10.

DIRECTIONS: Questions 4 through 10 are to be answered SOLELY on the basis of the following passage.

Job evaluation and job rating systems are intended to introduce scientific procedures. Any type of approach, when properly used, will give satisfactory results. The Point System, when properly validated by actual use, is more likely to be suitable for general use than the ranking system. In many aspects, the Factor Comparison Plan is a point system tied to money values. Of course, there may be another system that combines the ranking system with the point system, especially during the initial stages of the development of the program. After the program has been in use for some time, the tendency is to drop off the ranking phase and continue the use of the point system.

In the ranking system of rating of jobs, every job within the plant is arranged in some order, either from the one with the simplest qualifications to the one with maximum requirements, or in the reverse order. This system should be preceded by careful job analysis and the writing of accurate job descriptions before the rating process is undertaken. It is possible, of course, to take the jobs as they are found in the business enterprise and use the names as they are without any attempt at standardization, and merely rank them according to the general overall impression of the raters. Such a procedure is certain to fall short of what may reasonably be expected of job rating. Another procedure that is in reality merely a modification of the simple rating described above is to establish a series of grades or zones and arrange all he jobs in the plant into groups within these grades and zones. The practice in most common use is to arrange all the jobs in the plant according to their requirements by rating them and then to establish the classification or groups.

The actual ranking of jobs may be done by one individual, several individuals, or a committee. If several individuals are working independently on the task, it will usually be found that, in general, they agree but that their rankings vary in certain details. A conference between the individuals, with each person giving his reasons why he rated one way or another, usually produces agreement. The detailed job descriptions are particularly helpful when there is disagreement among raters as to the rating of certain jobs. It is not only possible but desirable to have workers participate in the construction of the job description and in rating the job.

4. The MAIN theme of this passage is
   A. the elimination of bias in job rating
   B. the rating of jobs by the ranking system
   C. the need or accuracy in allocating points in the point system
   D. pitfalls to avoid in selecting key jobs in the Factor Comparison Plan

4._____

5. The ranking system of rating jobs consists MAINLY of
   A. attaching a point value to each ratable factor of each job prior to establishing an equitable pay scale
   B. arranging every job in the organization in descending order and then following this up with a job analysis of the key jobs
   C. preparing accurate job descriptions after a job analysis and then arranging all jobs either in ascending or descending order based on job requirements
   D. arbitrarily establishing a hierarchy of job classes and grades and then fitting each job into a specific class and grade based on the opinions of unit supervisors

6. The above passage states that the system of classifying jobs MOST used in an organization is to
   A. organize all jobs in the organization in accordance with their requirements and then create categories or clusters of jobs
   B. classify all jobs in the organization according to the titles and rank by which they are currently known in the organization
   C. establish a pre-arranged series of grades or zones and then fit all jobs into one of the grades or zones
   D. determine the salary currently being paid for each job and then rank the jobs in order according to salary

7. According to the above passage, experience has shown that when a group of raters is assigned to the job evaluation task and each individual rates independently of the others, the raters GENERALLY
   A. *agree* with respect to all aspects of their rankings
   B. *disagree* with respect to all or nearly all aspects of the rankings
   C. *disagree* on overall ratings, but agree on specific rating factors
   D. *agree* on overall rankings, but have some variance in some details

8. The above passage states that the use of a detailed job description is of special value when
   A. employees of an organization have participated in the preliminary step involved in actual preparation of the job description
   B. labor representatives are not participating in ranking of the jobs
   C. an individual rater who is unsure of himself is ranking the jobs
   D. a group of raters is having difficulty reaching unanimity with respect to ranking a certain job

9. A comparison of the various rating systems as described in the above passage shows that
   A. the ranking system is not as appropriate for general use as a properly validated point system
   B. the point system is the same as the Factor Comparison Plan except that it places greater emphasis on money

C. no system is capable of combining the point system and the Factor Comparison Plan
D. the point system will be discontinued last when used in combination with the Factor comparison System

10. The above passage implies that the PRINCIPAL reason for creating job evaluation and rating systems was to help
   A. overcome union opposition to existing salary plans
   B. base wage determination on a more objective and orderly foundation
   C. eliminate personal bias on the part of the trained scientific job evaluators
   D. management determine if it was overpricing the various jobs in the organizational hierarchy

Questions 11-13.

DIRECTIONS: Questions 11 through 13 are to be answered SOLELY on the basis of the following passage.

The common sense character of the merit system seems so natural to most Americans that many people wonder why it should ever have been inoperative. After all, the American economic system, the most phenomenal the world has ever known, is also founded on a rugged selective process which emphasizes the personal qualities of capacity, industriousness, and productivity. The criteria may not have always been appropriate and competition has not always been fair, but competition there was, and the responsibilities and the rewards—with exceptions, of course—have gone to those who could measure up in terms of intelligence, knowledge, or perseverance. This has been true not only in the economic area, in the money-making process, but also in achievement in the professions and other walks of life.

11. According to the above passage, economic rewards in the United State have
   A. always been based on appropriate, fair criteria
   B. only recently been based on a competitive system
   C. not going to people who compete too ruggedly
   D. usually gone to those people with intelligence, knowledge, and perseverance

12. According to the above passage, a merit system is
   A. an unfair criterion on which to base rewards
   B. unnatural to anyone who is not American
   C. based only on common sense
   D. based on the same principles as the American economic system

13. According to the above passage, it is MOST accurate to say that
   A. the United States has always had a civil service merit system
   B. civil service employees are very rugged
   C. the American economic system has always been based on a merit objective
   D. competition is unique to the American way of life

Questions 14-15.

DIRECTIONS: Questions 14 and 15 are to be answered SOLELY on the basis of the following passage.

In-basket tests are often used to assess managerial potential. The exercise consists of a set of papers that would be likely to be found in the in-basket of an administrator or manager at any given time, and requires the individuals participating in the examination to indicate how they would dispose of each item found in the in-basket. In order to handle the in-basket effectively, they must successfully manage their time, refer and assign some work to subordinates, juggle potentially conflicting appointments and meetings, and arrange for follow-up of problems generated by the items in the in-basket. In other words, the in-basket test is attempting to evaluate the participants' abilities to organize their work, set priorities, delegate, control, and make decisions.

14. According to the above passage, to succeed in an in-basket test, an administrator must
    A. be able to read very quickly
    B. have a great deal of technical knowledge
    C. know when to delegate work
    D. arrange a lot of appointments and meetings

14._____

15. According to the above passage, all of the following abilities are indications of managerial potential EXCEPT the ability to
    A. organize and control
    B. manage time
    C. write effective reports
    D. make appropriate decisions

15._____

Questions 16-19.

DIRECTIONS: Questions 16 through 19 are to be answered SOLELY on the basis of the following passage.

A personnel researcher has at his disposal various approaches for obtaining information, analyzing it, and arriving at conclusions that have value in predicting and affecting the behavior of people at work. The type of method to be used depends on such factors as the nature of the research problem, the available data, and the attitudes of those people being studied to the various kinds of approaches. While the experimental approach, with its use of control groups, is the most refined type of study, there are others that are often found useful in personnel research. Surveys, in which the researcher obtains facts on a problem from a variety of sources, are employed in research on wages, fringe benefits, and labor relations. Historical studies are used to trace the development of problems in order to understand them better and to isolate possible causative factors. Case studies are generally developed to explore all the details of a particular problem that is representative of other similar problems. A researcher chooses the most appropriate form of study for the problem he is investigating. He should recognize, however, that the experimental method, commonly referred to as the scientific method, if used validly and reliably, gives the most conclusive results.

16. The above passage discusses several approaches used to obtain information on particular problems.
    Which of the following may be MOST reasonably concluded from the passage? A(n)
    A. historical study cannot determine causative factors
    B. survey is often used in research on fringe benefits
    C. case study is usually used to explore a problem that is unique and unrelated to other problems
    D. experimental study is used when the scientific approach to a problem fails

17. According to the above passage, all of the following are factors that may determine the type of approach a researcher uses EXCEPT
    A. the attitudes of people toward being used in control groups
    B. the number of available sources
    C. his desire to isolate possible causative factors
    D. the degree of accuracy he requires

18. The words *scientific method*, as used in the last sentence of the above passage, refer to a type of study which, according to the above passage
    A. uses a variety of sources
    B. traces the development of problems
    C. uses control groups
    D. analyzes the details of a representative problem

19. Which of the following can be MOST reasonably concluded from the above passage?
    In obtaining and analyzing information on a particular problem, a researcher employs the method which is the
    A. most accurate
    B. most suitable
    C. least expensive
    D. least time-consuming

Questions 20-25.

DIRECTIONS: Questions 20 through 25 are to be answered SOLELY on the basis of the following passage.

The quality of the voice of a worker is an important factor in conveying to clients and co-workers his attitude and, to some degree, his character. The human voice, when not consciously disguised, may reflect a person's mood, temper, and personality. It has been shown in several experiments that certain character traits can be assessed with better than chance accuracy through listening to the voice of an unknown person who cannot be seen.

Since one of the objectives of the worker is to put clients at ease and to present an encouraging and comfortable atmosphere, a harsh, shrill, or loud voice could have a negative effect. A client who displays emotions of anger or resentment would probably be provoked even further by a caustic tone. In a face-to-face situation, an unpleasant voice may be compensated for, to some degree, by a concerned and kind facial expression. However, when one speaks on the telephone, the expression on one's face cannot be seen by the listener. A supervising clerk who wishes to represent himself effectively to clients should try to eliminate as many faults as possible in striving to develop desirable voice qualities.

20. If a worker uses a sarcastic tone while interviewing a resentful client, the client, according to the above passage, would MOST likely
    A. avoid the face-to-face problem
    B. be ashamed of his behavior
    C. become more resentful
    D. be provoked to violence

21. According to the passage, experiments comparing voice and character traits have demonstrated that
    A. prospects for improving an unpleasant voice through training are better than chance
    B. the voice can be altered to project many different psychological characteristics
    C. the quality of the human voice reveals more about the speaker than his words do
    D. the speaker's voice tells the hearer something about the speaker's personality

22. Which of the following, according to the above passage, is a person's voice MOST likely to reveal?
    His
    A. prejudices
    B. intelligence
    C. social awareness
    D. temperament

23. It may be MOST reasonably concluded from the above passage that an interested and sympathetic expression on the face of a worker
    A. may induce a client to feel certain he will receive welfare benefits
    B. will eliminate the need for pleasant vocal qualities in the interviewer
    C. may help to make up for an unpleasant voice in the interviewer
    D. is desirable as the interviewer speaks on the telephone to a client

24. Of the following, the MOST reasonable implication of the above paragraph is that a worker should, when speaking to a client, control and use his voice to
    A. simulate a feeling of interest in the problems of the client
    B. express his emotions directly and adequately
    C. help produce in the client a sense of comfort and security
    D. reflect his own true personality

25. It may be concluded from the above passage that the PARTICULAR reason for a worker to pay special attention to modulating her voice when talking on the phone to a client is that, during a telephone conversation
    A. there is a necessity to compensate for the way in which a telephone distorts the voice
    B. the voice of the worker is a reflection of her mood and character
    C. the client can react only on the basis of the voice and words she hears
    D. the client may have difficulty getting a clear understanding over the telephone

KEY (CORRECT ANSWERS)

1.	D		11.	D
2.	B		12.	D
3.	B		13.	C
4.	B		14.	C
5.	C		15.	C
6.	A		16.	B
7.	D		17.	D
8.	D		18.	C
9.	A		19.	B
10.	B		20.	C

21. D
22. D
23. C
24. C
25. C

TEST 2

DIRECTIONS: Each question or incomplete statement is followed by several suggested answers or completions. Select the one that BEST answers the question or completes the statement. *PRINT THE LETTER OF THE CORRECT ANSWER IN THE SPACE AT THE RIGHT.*

Questions 1-3.

DIRECTIONS: Questions 1 through 3 are to be answered SOLELY on the basis of the following paragraph.

Suppose you are given the job of printing, collating, and stapling 8,000 copies of a ten-page booklet as soon as possible. You have available one photo-offset machine, a collator with an automatic stapler, and the personnel to operate these machines. All will be available for however long the job takes to complete. The photo-offset machine prints 5,000 impressions an hour, and it takes about 15 minutes to set up a plate. The collator, including time for insertion of pages and stapling, can process about 2,000 booklets an hour. (Answers should be based on the assumption that there are no breakdowns or delays.)

1. Assuming that all the printing is finished before the collating is started, if the job is given to you late Monday and your section can begin work the next day and is able to devote seven hours a day, Monday through Friday, to the job until it is finished, what is the BEST estimate of when the job will be finished?
   A. Wednesday afternoon of the same week
   B. Thursday morning of the same week
   C. Friday morning of the same week
   D. Monday morning of the next week

1.____

2. An operator suggests to you that instead of completing all the printing and then beginning collating and stapling, you first print all the pages for 4,000 booklets, so that they can be collated and stapled while the last 4,000 pages are being printed.
   If you accepted this suggestion, the job would be completed
   A. sooner but would require more man-hours
   B at the same time using either method
   C. later and would require more man-hours
   D. sooner but there would be more wear and tear on the plates

2.____

3. Assume that you have the same assignment and equipment as described above, but 16,000 copies of the booklet are needed instead of 8,000.
   If you decided to print 8,000 complete booklets, then collate and staple them while you started printing the next 8,000 booklets, which of the following statements would MOST accurately describe the relationship between this new method and your original method of printing all the booklets at one time, and then collating and stapling them? The
   A. job would be completed at the same time regardless of the method used
   B. new method would result in the job's being completed 3½ hours earlier
   C. original method would result in the job's being completed an hour later
   D. new method would result in the job's being completed 1½ hours earlier

3.____

87

Questions 4-6.

DIRECTIONS: Questions 4 through 6 are to be answered SOLELY on the basis of the following passage.

When using words like company, association, council, committee, and board in place of the full official name, the writer should not capitalize these short forms unless he intends them to invoke the full force of the institution's authority. In legal contracts, in minutes, or in formal correspondence where one is speaking formally and officially on behalf of the company, the term Company is usually capitalized, but in ordinary usage, where it is not essential to load the short form with this significance, capitalization would be excessive. (Example: The company will have many good openings for graduates this June.)

The treatment recommended for short forms of place names is essentially the same as that recommended for short forms of organizational names. In general, we capitalize the full form but not the short form. If Park Avenue is referred to in one sentence, then the *avenue* is sufficient in subsequent references. The same is true with words like building, hotel, station, and airport, which are capitalized when part of a proper name changed (Pan Am Building, Hotel Plaza, Union Station, O'Hare Airport), but are simply lower-cased when replacing these specific names.

4. The above passage states that USUALLY the short forms of names of organizations
    A. and places should not be capitalized
    B. and places should be capitalized
    C. should not be capitalized, but the short forms of names of places should be capitalized
    D. should be capitalized, but the short forms of names of places should not be capitalized

    4._____

5. The above passage states that in legal contracts, in minutes, and in formal correspondence, the short forms of names of organizations should
    A. usually not be capitalized   B. usually be capitalized
    C. usually not be used   D. never be used

    5._____

6. It can be inferred from the above passage that decisions regarding when to capitalize certain words
    A. should be left to the discretion of the writer
    B. should be based on generally accepted rules
    C. depend on the total number of words capitalized
    D. are of minor importance

    6._____

Questions 7-10.

DIRECTIONS: Questions 7 through 10 are to be answered SOLELY on the basis of the following passage.

Use of the systems and procedures approach to office management is revolutionizing the supervision of office work. This approach views an enterprise as an entity which seeks to fulfill definite objectives. Systems and procedures help to organize repetitive work into a routine, thus reducing the amount of decision making required for its accomplishment. As a result, employees are guided in their efforts and perform only necessary work. Supervisors are relieved of any details of execution and are free to attend to more important work. Establishing work guides which require that identical tasks be performed the same way each time permits standardization of forms, machine operations, work methods, and controls. This approach also reduces the probability of errors. Any error committed is usually discovered quickly because the incorrect work does not meet the requirement of the work guides. Errors are also reduced through work specialization, which allows each employee to become thoroughly proficient in a particular type of work. Such proficiency also tends to improve the morale of the employees.

7. The above passage states that the accuracy of an employee's work is INCREASED by
   A. using the work specialization approach
   B. employing a probability sample
   C. requiring him to shift at one time into different types of tasks
   D. having his supervisor check each detail of work execution

8. Of the following, which one BEST expresses the main theme of the above passage? The
   A. advantages and disadvantages of the systems and procedures approach to office management
   B. effectiveness of the systems and procedures approach to office management in developing skills
   C. systems and procedures approach to office management as it relates to office costs
   D. advantages of the systems and procedures approach to office management for supervisors and office workers

9. Work guides are LEAST likely to be used when
   A. standardized forms are used
   B. a particular office task is distinct and different from all others
   C. identical tasks are to be performed in identical ways
   D. similar work methods are expected from each employee

10. According to the above passage, when an employee makes a work error, it USUALLY
    A. is quickly corrected by the supervisor
    B. necessitates a change in the work guides
    C. can be detected quickly if work guides are in use
    D. increases the probability of further errors by that employee

Questions 11-12.

DIRECTIONS: Questions 11 and 12 are to be answered SOLELY on the basis of the following passage.

The coordination of the many activities of a large public agency is absolutely essential. Coordination, as an administrative principle, must be distinguished from and is independent of cooperation. Coordination can be of either the horizontal or the vertical type. In large organizations, the objectives of vertical coordination are achieved by the transmission of orders and statements of policy down through the various levels of authority. It is an accepted generalization that the more authoritarian the organization, the more easily may vertical coordination be accomplished. Horizontal coordination is arrived through staff work, administrative management, and conferences of administrators of equal rank. It is obvious that of the two types of coordination, the vertical kind is more important, for at best horizontal coordination only supplements the coordination effected up and down the line,

11. According to the above passage, the ease with which vertical coordination is achieved in a large agency depends upon
    A. the extent to which control is firmly exercised from above
    B. the objectives that have been established for the agency
    C. the importance attached by employees to the orders and statements of policy transmitted through the agency
    D. the cooperation obtained at the various levels of authority

12. According to the above passage,
    A. vertical coordination is dependent for its success upon horizontal coordination
    B. one type of coordination may work in opposition to the other
    C. similar methods may be used to achieve both types of coordination
    D. horizontal coordination is at most an addition to vertical coordination

Questions 13-17.

DIRECTIONS: Questions 13 through 17 are to be answered SOLELY on the basis of the following situation.

Assume that you are a newly appointed supervisor in the same unit in which you have been acting as a provisional for some time. You have in your unit the following workers:

WORKER I: He has always been an efficient worker. In a number of his cases, the clients have recently begun to complain that they cannot manage on the departmental budget.

WORKER II: He has been under selective supervision for some time as an experienced, competent worker. He now begins to be late for his supervisory conferences and to stress how much work he has to do.

WORKER III: He has been making considerable improvement in his ability to handle the details of his job. He now tells you, during an individual conference, that he does not need such close supervision and that he wants to operate more independently. He says that Worker II is always available when he needs a little information or help but, in general, he can manage very well by himself.

5 (#2)

WORKER IV: He brings you a complex case for decision as to eligibility. Discussion of the case brings out the fact that he has failed to consider all the available resources adequately but has stressed the family's needs to include every extra item in the budget. This is the third case of a similar nature that his worker has brought to you recently. This worker and Worker I work in adjacent territory and are rather friendly.

In the following questions, select the option that describes the method of dealing with these workers that illustrate BEST supervisory practice.

13. With respect to supervision of Worker I, the assistant supervisor should 13._____
    A. discuss with the worker, in an individual conference, any problems that he may be having due to the increase in the cost of living
    B. plan a group conference for the unit around budgeting, as both Workers I and IV seem to be having budgetary difficulties
    C. discuss with Workers I and IV together the meaning of money as acceptance or rejection to the clients
    D. discuss with Worker I the budgetary data in each case in relation to each client's situation

14. With respect to supervision of Worker II, the supervisory should 14._____
    A. move slowly with this worker and give him time to learn that the supervisor's official appointment has not changed his attitudes or methods of supervision
    B. discuss the worker's change of attitude and asks him to analyze the reasons for his change in behavior
    C. take time to show the worker how he is avoiding his responsibility in the supervisor-worker relationship and that he is resisting supervision
    D. hold an evaluatory conference with the worker and show him how he is taking over responsibilities that are not his by providing supervision for Worker III

15. With respect to supervision of Worker III, the supervisor should discuss with this worker 15._____
    A. why he would rather have supervision from Worker II than from the supervisor
    B. the necessity for further improvement before he can go on selective supervision
    C. an analysis of the improvement that has been made and the extent to which the worker is able to handle the total job for which he is responsible
    D. the responsibility of the supervisor to see that clients receive adequate service

16. With respect to supervision of Worker IV, the supervisor should 16._____
    A. show the worker that resources figures are incomplete but that even if they were complete, the family would probably be eligible for assistance
    B. ask the worker why he is so protective of these families since there are three cases so similar

C. discuss with the worker all three cases at the same time so that the worker may see his own role in the three situations
D. discuss with the worker the reasons for departmental policies and procedures around budgeting

17. With respect to supervision of Workers I and IV, since these two workers are friends and would seem to be influencing each other, the supervisor should
    A. hold a joint conference with them both, pointing out how they should clear with the supervisor and not make their own rules together
    B. handle the problems of each separately in individual conferences
    C. separate them by transferring one to another territory or another unit
    D. take up the problem of workers asking help of each other rather than from the supervisor in a group meeting

17.____

Questions 18-20.

DIRECTIONS: Questions 18 through 20 are to be answered SOLELY on the basis of the following passage.

One of the key supervisory problems in a large municipal recreation department is that many leaders are assigned to isolated playgrounds or small centers, where it is difficult to observe their work regularly. Often their facilities are extremely limited. In such settings, as well as in larger recreation centers, where many recreation leaders tend to have other jobs as well, there tends to be a low level of morale and incentive. Still, it is the supervisor's task to help recreation personnel to develop pride in their work and to maintain a high level of performance. With isolated leaders, the supervisor may give advice or assistance. Leaders may be assigned to different tasks or settings during the year to maximize their productivity and provide new challenges. When it is clear that leaders are no willing to make a real effort to contribute to the department, the possibility of penalties must be considered, within the scope of departmental policy and the union contract. However, the supervisor should be constructive, encourage and assist workers to take a greater interest in their work, be innovative, and try to raise morale and to improve performance in positive ways.

18. The one of the following that would the MOST appropriate title for the above passage is
    A. Small Community Centers – Pro and Con
    B. Planning Better Recreation Programs
    C. The Supervisor's Task in Upgrading Personnel Performance
    D. The Supervisor and the Municipal Union – Rights and Obligations

18.____

19. The above passage makes clear that recreation leadership performance in all recreation playgrounds and centers throughout a large city is
    A. generally above average, with good morale on the part of most recreation leaders
    B. beyond description since no one has ever observed or evaluated recreation leaders

19.____

C. a key test of the personnel department's effort to develop more effective hiring standards
D. of mixed quality, with many recreation leaders having poor morale and a low level of achievement

20. According to the above passage, the supervisor's role is to 20.____
    A. use disciplinary action as his major tool in upgrading performance
    B. tolerate the lack of effort of individual employees since they are assigned to isolated playgrounds or small centers
    C. employ encouragement, advice, and, when appropriate, disciplinary action to improve performance
    D. inform the county supervisor whenever malfeasance or idleness is detected

Questions 21-25.

DIRECTIONS: Questions 21 through 25 are to be answered SOLELY on the basis of the following passage.

EMPLOYEE LEAVE REGULATIONS

Peter Smith, as a full-time permanent city employee under the Career and Salary Plan, earns an *annual leave allowance*. This consists of a certain number of days off a year with pay and may be used for vacation, personal business, and for observing religious holidays. As a newly appointed employee, during his first 8 years of city service, he will earn an annual leave allowance of 20 days off a year (an average of $1^{2}/_{3}$ days off a month). After he has finished 8 full years of working for the city, he will begin earning an additional 5 days off a year. His annual leave allowance, therefore, will then be 25 days a year and will remain at this amount for seven full years. He will begin earning an additional two days off a year at this amount for seven full years. He will begin earning an additional two days off a year after he has completed a total of 15 years of city employment. Therefore, in his sixteenth year of working for the city, Mr. Smith will be earning 27 days off a year as his annual leave allowance (an average of $2^{1}/_{4}$ days off a month).

A *sick leave allowance* of one day a month is also given to Mr. Smith, but it can be used only in cases of actual illness. When Mr. Smith returns to work after using sick leave allowance, he must have a doctor's note if the absence is for a total of more than 3 days, but he may also be required to show a doctor's note for absences of 1, 2, or 3 days.

21. According to the above passage, Mr. Smith's annual leave allowance consists 21.____
    of a certain number of days off a year which he
    A. does not get paid for
    B. gets paid for at time and a half
    C. may use for personal business
    D. may not use for observing religious holidays

22. According to the above passage, after Mr. Smith has been working for the city 22.____
    for 9 years, his annual leave allowance will be _____ days a year.
    A. 20   B. 25   C. 27   D. 37

23. According to the above passage, Mr. Smith will begin earning an average of 2 days off a month as his annual leave allowance after he has worked for the city for _____ full years.
    A. 7   B. 8   C. 15   D. 17

24. According to the above passage, Mr. Smith is given a sick leave allowance of
    A. 1 day every 2 months
    B. 1 day per month
    C. 1$\frac{2}{3}$ days per month
    D. 2¼ days a month

25. According to the above passage, when he uses sick leave allowance, Mr. Smith may be required to show a doctor's note
    A. even if his absence is for only 1 day
    B. only if his absence is for more than 2 days
    C. only if his absence is for more than 3 days
    D. only if his absence is for 3 days or more

KEY (CORRECT ANSWERS)

1.	C	11.	A
2.	C	12.	D
3.	D	13.	D
4.	A	14.	A
5.	B	15.	C
6.	B	16.	C
7.	A	17.	B
8.	D	18.	C
9.	B	19.	D
10.	C	20.	C

21.	C
22.	B
23.	C
24.	B
25.	A

TEST 3

DIRECTIONS: Each question or incomplete statement is followed by several suggested answers or completions. Select the one that BEST answers the question or completes the statement. *PRINT THE LETTER OF THE CORRECT ANSWER IN THE SPACE AT THE RIGHT.*

Questions 1-6.

DIRECTIONS: Questions 1 through 6 are to be answered SOLELY on the basis of the following passage.

    A folder is made of a sheet of heavy paper (manila, kraft, pressboard, or red rope stock) that has been folded once so that the back is about one-half inch higher than the front. Folders are larger than the papers they contain in order to protect them. Two standard folder sizes are *letter size* for papers that are 8½" x 11" and *legal cap* for papers that are 8½" x 13".
    Folders are cut across the top in two ways: so that the back is straight (straight-cut) or so that the back has a tab that projects above the top of the folder. Such tabs bear captions that identify the contents of each folder. Tabs vary in width and position. The tabs of a set of folders that are *one-half cut* are half the width of the folder and have only two positions.
    One-third cut folders have three positions, each tab occupying a third of the width of the folder. Another standard tabbing is *one-fifth cut*, which has five positions. There are also folders with *two-fifths cut*, with the tabs in the third and fourth or fourth and fifth positions.

1. Of the following, the BEST title for the above passage is
    A. Filing Folders
    B. Standard Folder Sizes
    C. The Uses of the Folder
    D. The Use of Tabs

2. According to the above passage, one of the standard folder sizes is called
    A. Kraft cut
    B. legal cap
    C. one-half cut
    D. straight-cut

3. According to the above passage, tabs are GENERALLY placed along the _____ of the folder.
    A. back   B. front   C. left side   D. right side

4. According to the above passage, a tab is GENERALLY used to
    A. distinguish between standard folder sizes
    B. identify the contents of a folder
    C. increase the size of the folder
    D. protect the papers within the folder

5. According to the above passage, a folder that is two-fifths cut has _____ tabs.
    A. no   B. two   C. three   D. five

6. According to the above passage, one reason for making folders larger than the papers they contain is that
   A. only a certain size folder can be made from heavy paper
   B. they will protect the papers
   C. they will aid in setting up a tab system
   D. the back of the folder must be higher than the front

Questions 7-15.

DIRECTIONS: Questions 7 through 15 are to be answered SOLELY on the basis of the following passage.

The City University of New York traces its origins to 1847, when the Free Academy, which later became City College, was founded as the first tuition-free municipal college. City and Hunter Colleges were placed under the direction of the Board of Higher Education in 1926, and Brooklyn and Queens Colleges were subsequently added to the system of municipal colleges. In 1955, Staten Island Community College, the first of the two-year colleges sponsored by the Board of Higher Education under the program of the State University of New York, joined the system.

In 1961, the four senior colleges and three community colleges then under the jurisdiction of the Board of Higher Education became the City University of New York, and a University Graduate Division was organized to offer programs leading to the Ph.D. Since then, the university has undergone even more rapid growth. Today, it consists of nine senior colleges, an upper division college which admits students at the junior level, eight community colleges, a graduate division, and an affiliated medical center.

In the summer of 1969, the Board of Higher Education resolved that the time had come to commit the resources of the university to meeting an urgent social need—unrestricted access to higher education for all youths of the City. Determined to prevent the waste of human potential represented by the thousands of high school graduates whose limited educational opportunities left them unable to meet existing admission standards, the Board moved to adopt a policy of Open Admissions. It was their judgment that the best way of determining whether a potential student can benefit from college work is to admit him to college, provide him with the learning assistance he needs, and then evaluate his performance.

Beginning with the class of June 1970, every New York City resident who received a high school diploma from a public or private high school was guaranteed a place in one of the colleges of City University.

7. Of the following, the BEST title for the above passage is
   A. A Brief History of the City University
   B. High Schools and the City University
   C. The Components of the University
   D. Tuition-free Colleges

8. According to the above passage, which one of the following colleges of the City University was ORIGINALLY called the Free Academy?
   A. Brooklyn College   B. City College
   C. Hunter College   D. Queens College

9. According to the above passage, the system of municipal colleges became the City University of New York in
   A. 1926   B. 1955   C. 1961   D. 1969

10. According to the above passage, Staten Island Community College came under the jurisdiction of the Board of Higher Education
    A. 6 years after a Graduate Division was organized
    B. 8 years before the adoption of the Open Admissions Policy
    C. 29 years after Brooklyn and Queens Colleges
    D. 29 years after City and Hunter Colleges

11. According to the above passage, the Staten Island Community College is
    A. a graduate division center   B. a senior college
    C. a two-year college   D. an upper division college

12. According to the above passage, the TOTAL number of colleges, divisions, and affiliated branches of the City University is
    A. 18   B. 19   C. 20   D. 21

13. According to the above passage, the Open Admissions Policy is designed to determine whether a potential student will benefit from college by PRIMARILY
    A. discouraging competition for placement in the City University among high school students
    B. evaluating his performance after entry into college
    C. lowering admission standards
    D. providing learning assistance before entry into college

14. According to the above passage, the FIRST class to be affected by the Open Admissions Policy was the
    A. high school class which graduated in January 1970
    B. City University class which graduated in June 1970
    C. high school class when graduated in June 1970
    D. City University class when graduated in June 1970

15. According to the above passage, one of the reasons that the Board of Higher Education initiated the policy of Open Admission was to
    A. enable high school graduates with a background of limited educational opportunities to enter college
    B. expand the growth of the City University so as to increase the number and variety of degrees offered
    C. provide a social resource to the qualified youth of the City
    D. revise admission standards to meet the needs of the City

Questions 16-18.

DIRECTIONS: Questions 16 through 18 are to be answered SOLELY on the basis of the following passage.

Hereafter, all probationary students interested in transferring to community college career programs (associate degrees) from liberal arts programs in senior colleges (bachelor degrees) will be eligible for such transfers if they have completed no more than three semesters.
For students with averages 1.5 or above, transfer will be automatic. Those with 1.0 to 1.5 averages can transfer provisionally and will be required to make substantial progress during the first semester in the career program. Once transfer has taken place, only those courses in which passing grades were received will be computed in the community college grade-point average.
No request for transfer will be accepted from probationary students wishing to enter the liberal arts programs at the community college.

16. According to the above passage, the one of the following which is the BEST statement concerning the transfer of probationary students is that a probationary student
    A. may transfer to a career program at the end of one semester
    B. must complete three semester hours before he is eligible for transfer
    C. is not eligible to transfer to a career program
    D. is eligible to transfer to a liberal arts program

17. Which of the following is the BEST statement of academic evaluation for transfer purposes in the case of probationary students?
    A. No probationary student with an average under 1.5 may transfer.
    B. A probationary student with an average of 1.3 may not transfer.
    C. A probationary student with an average of 1.6 may transfer.
    D. A probationary student with an average of .8 may transfer on a provisional basis.

18. It is MOST likely that, of the following, the next degree sought by one who already holds the Associate in Science degree would be a(n) _____ degree.
    A. Assistantship in Science   B. Associate in Applied Science
    C. Bachelor of Science   D. Doctor of Philosophy

Questions 19-20.

DIRECTIONS: Questions 19 and 20 are to be answered SOLELY on the basis of the following passage.

Auto: Auto travel requires prior approval by the President and/or appropriate Dean and must be indicated in the *Request for Travel Authorization* form. Employees authorized to use personal autos on official College business will be reimbursed at the rate of 28¢ per mile for the first 500 miles driven and 18¢ per mile for mileage driven in excess of 500 mile. The Comptroller's Office may limit the amount of reimbursement to the expenditure that would have been made if a less expensive mode of transportation (railroad, airplane, bus, etc.) had been utilized. If this occurs, the traveler will have to pick up the excess expenditure as a personal expense.

Tolls, Parking Fees, and Parking Meter Fees are not reimbursable and many not be claimed.

19. Suppose that Professor T gives the office assistant the following memorandum: Used car for official trip to Albany, New York, and return. Distance from New York to Albany is 148 miles. Tolls were $3.50 each way. Parking garage cost $3.00. When preparing the Travel Expense Voucher for Professor T, the figure which should be claimed for transportation is
    A. $120.88   B. $113.88   C. $82.88   D. $51.44

    19._____

20. Suppose that Professor V gives the office assistant the following memorandum: Used car for official trip to Pittsburgh, Pennsylvania, and return. Distance from New York to Pittsburgh is 350 miles. Tolls were $3.30, $11.40 going, and $3.30, $2.00 returning.
    When preparing the Travel Expense Voucher for Professor V, the figure which should be claimed for transportation is
    A. $225.40   B. $176.00   C. $127.40   D. $98.00

    20._____

Questions 21-25.

DIRECTIONS: Questions 21 through 25 are to be answered SOLELY on the basis of the following passage.

For a period of nearly fifteen years, beginning in the mid-1950's, higher education sustained a phenomenal rate of growth. The factor principally responsible were continuing improvement in the rate of college entrance by high school graduates, a 50 percent increase in the size of the college-age (eighteen to twenty-one) group and—until about 1967—a rapid expansion of university research activity supported by the Federal government.

Today, as one looks ahead to the year 2010, it is apparent that each of these favorable stimuli will either be abated or turn into a negative factor. The rate of growth of the college-age group has already diminished; and from 2000 to 2005, the size of the college-age group has shrunk annually almost as fast as it grew from 1965 to 1970. From 2005 to 2010, this annual decrease will slow down so that by 2010 the age group will be about the same size as it was in 2009. This substantial net decrease in the size of the college-age group (from 1995 to 2010) will dramatically affect college enrollments since, currently, 83 percent of undergraduates are twenty-one and under, and another 11 percent are twenty-to to twenty-four.

21. Which one of the following factors is NOT mentioned in the above passage as contributing to the high rate of growth of higher education?
    A. A large increase in the size of the eighteen to twenty-one age group
    B. The equalization of educational opportunities among socio-economic groups
    C. The Federal budget impact on research and development spending in the higher education sector
    D. The increasing rate at which high school graduates enter college

    21._____

22. Based on the information in the above passage, the size of the college-age group in 2010 will be
    A. larger than it was in 2009
    B. larger than it was in 1995
    C. smaller than it was in 2005
    D. about the same as it was in 2000

23. According to the above passage, the tremendous rate of growth of higher education started around
    A. 1950   B. 1955   C. 1960   D. 1965

24. The percentage of undergraduates who are over age 24 is MOST NEARLY
    A. 6%   B. 8%   C. 11%   D. 17%

25. Which one of the following conclusions can be substantiated by the information given in the above passage?
    A. The college-age group was about the same size in 2000 as it was in 1965.
    B. The annual decrease in the size of the college-age group from 2000 to 2005 is about the same as the annual increase from 1965 to 1970.
    C. The overall decrease in the size of the college-age group from 2000 to 2005 will be followed by an overall increase in its size from 2005 to 2010.
    D. The size of the college-age group is decreasing at a fairly constant rate from 1995 to 2010.

KEY (CORRECT ANSWERS)

1.	A	11.	C
2.	B	12.	C
3.	A	13.	B
4.	B	14.	C
5.	B	15.	A
6.	B	16.	A
7.	A	17.	C
8.	B	18.	C
9.	C	19.	C
10.	D	20.	B

21. B
22. C
23. B
24. A
25. B

EXAMINATION SECTION
TEST 1

DIRECTIONS: Each question or incomplete statement is followed by several suggested answers or completions. Select the one that BEST answers the question or completes the statement. *PRINT THE LETTER OF THE CORRECT ANSWER IN THE SPACE AT THE RIGHT.*

1. Suppose that one of the forms you fill out daily requires some information which you know is unnecessary.
   Which is the BEST action to take?
   A. Refuse to supply the information you think is unnecessary.
   B. Continue to fill out the form as required, even though the information is unnecessary.
   C. Suggest to your supervisor that the form be revised to reflect useful information.
   D. Suggest that fewer copies of the form be required.

   1.____

2. Of the following, the MOST likely reason for recommending that your department establish a standard form for recording certain information would be that this information
   A. will be produced at some disciplinary hearing
   B. concerns a secret or confidential record about an unusual incident at the garage
   C. contains a detailed explanation of a complex procedure
   D. must be taken from a large number of people on a regular basis

   2.____

3. If the four steps listed below for processing records were given in logical sequence, the one that would be the THIRD step is
   A. coding the records, using a chart or classification system
   B. inspecting the records to make sure they have been released for filing
   C. preparing cross-reference sheets or cards
   D. skimming the records to determine filing captions

   3.____

4. Which of the following BEST describes "office work simplification"?
   A. An attempt to increase the rate of production by speeding up the movements of employees
   B. Eliminating wasteful steps in order to increase efficiency
   C. Making jobs as easy as possible for employees so they will not be overworked
   D. Eliminating all difficult tasks from an office and leaving only simple ones

   4.____

5. The use of the same method of recordkeeping and reporting by all sections is
   A. *desirable*, mainly because it saves time in section operations
   B. *undesirable*, mainly because it kills the initiative of the individual section foreman
   C. *desirable*, mainly because it will be easier for the superior to evaluate and compare section operations
   D. *undesirable*, mainly because operations vary from section to section and uniform recordkeeping and reporting is not appropriate

6. The GREATEST benefit the section officer will have from keeping complete and accurate records of section operations is that
   A. he will find it easier to run his section efficiently
   B. he will need less equipment
   C. he will need less manpower
   D. the section will run smoothly when he is out

7. You have prepared a report to your superior and are ready to send it forward. But on reading it, you think some parts are not clearly expressed and the superior may have difficulty getting your point.
   Of the following, it would be BEST for you to
   A. give the report to one of your men to read, and, if he has no trouble understanding it, send it through
   B. forward the report and call the superior the next day to ask if it was all right
   C. forward the report as is; higher echelons should be able to understand any report prepared by a section officer
   D. do the report over, re-writing the sections you are doubtful of

8. Of the following, a flow chart is BEST described as a chart which shows
   A. the places through which work moves in the course of the job process
   B. which employees perform specific functions leading to the completion of a job
   C. the schedules for production and how they eliminate waiting time between jobs
   D. how work units are affected by the actions of related work units

9. A superior decided to hold a problem-solving conference with his entire staff and distributed an announcement and agenda one week before the meeting.
   Of the following, the BEST reason for providing each participate with an agenda is that
   A. participants will feel that something will be accomplished
   B. participants may prepare for the conference
   C. controversy will be reduced
   D. the top man should state the expected conclusions

10. The one of the following activities which is generally the LEAST proper function of a centralized procedures section is
    A. issuing new and revised procedural instructions
    B. coordinating forms revision and procedural changes
    C. accepting or rejecting authorized procedural changes
    D. controlling standard numbering systems for procedural releases

    10.____

11. Assume that it is the policy of an operating unit to act on all requests received within five working days. Several operations are involved in acting on these requests. Each operation is performed by a separate sub-unit. The staff of the unit is reasonable adequate to handle this workload.
    If only one of the following can be done, the MOST effective procedure for maintaining adherence to the unit's five-day processing policy is to
    A. maintain a central "tickler" file in each sub-unit for the requests received daily in that sub-unit
    B. prepare a "tickler" card for each request and follow it up five days later to determine whether action has been taken
    C. rely on standards of production for each operation as an incentive to the employees of each sub-unit to meet the schedule
    D. schedule the operations on a timetable basis so that the request will be forwarded from one sub-unit to another within specified time limits

    11.____

12. When one or two simple changes are needed in a memo to another unit or in a letter to a citizen, a unit head follows the practice of making such simple changes neatly in ink.
    This practice is GENERALLY
    A. *poor*, chiefly because it reflects unfavorably on the originating unit's ability to make a decision
    B. *good*, chiefly because the department's public image is likely to be improved when people see it as trying to save money and speed up its processes
    C. *poor*, chiefly because a letter or document prepared in final form represents an investment of department time and effort and should go out only as a perfect finished product
    D. *good*, chiefly because the document may be important, and sending it back for retyping may delay it too long to achieve its purpose

    12.____

13. Suppose that one of the office machines in your unit is badly in need of replacement.
    Of the following, the MOST important reason for postponing immediate purchase of a new machine would be that
    A. a later model of the machine is expected on the market in a few months
    B. the new machine is more expensive than the old machine
    C. the operator of the present machine will have to be instructed by the manufacturer in the operation of the new machine
    D. the employee operating the old machine is not complaining

    13.____

14. To avoid cutting off parts of letters when using an automatic letter opener, it is BEST to
    A. arrange all of the letters so that the addresses are right side up
    B. hold the envelopes up to the light to make sure their contents have not settled to the side that is to be opened
    C. strike the envelopes against a table or desktop several times so that the contents of all the envelopes settle to one side
    D. check the enclosures periodically to make sure that the machine has not been cutting into them

15. Of the following, the BEST reason for setting up a partitioned work area for the typists in our office is that
    A. an uninterrupted flow of work among the typists will be possible
    B. complaints about ventilation and lighting will be reduced
    C. the first-line supervisor will have more direct control over the typists
    D. the noise of the typewriters will be less disturbing to other workers

16. From the viewpoint of use of a typewriter to fill in a form, the MOST important design factor to consider is
    A. standard spacing
    B. box headings
    C. serial numbering
    D. vertical guide lines

17. Requests to repair office equipment which appears to be unsafe should be given priority MAINLY because, if repairs are delayed,
    A. there may be injuries to staff
    B. there may be further deterioration of the equipment
    C. work flow may be interrupted
    D. the cost of repair may increase

18. A clerk is asked to complete two assignments – transcribe a handwritten business letter and create a spreadsheet. Which two computer programs would the clerk use?
    A. Microsoft Word and Microsoft Excel
    B. Microsoft Word and Microsoft PowerPoint
    C. Google Docs and Google Chrome
    D. Adobe Reader and Microsoft PowerPoint

19. Generally, the actual floor space occupied by a standard letter-size office file cabinet, when closed, is MOST NEARLY
    A. ½ square foot
    B. 3 square feet
    C. 7 square feet
    D. 11 square feet

20. Suppose a clerk under your supervision accidentally opens a personal letter while handling office mail.
    Under such circumstances, you should tell the clerk to put the letter back into the envelope and
    A. take the letter to the person to whom it belongs and make sure he understands that the clerk did not read it
    B. try to seal the envelope so it won't appear to have been opened

C. write on the envelope "Sorry – opened by mistake," and put his initials on it
D. write on the envelope "Sorry – opened by mistake," but not put his initials on it

21. Standard forms frequently call for entries on them to be printed. The MAIN reason for this practice is that printing, as compared to writing, is GENERALLY
    A. more compact
    B. more legal
    C. more legible
    D. easier to do

22. After a stenographer types a letter which has been dictated, the finished letter should be carefully read for errors.
    If he dictator follows the procedure of carefully reading each transcribed letter, a stenographer, under your supervision, should, unless you instruct her otherwise
    A. not take time to proofread transcribed letters
    B. continue to carefully proofread transcribed letters
    C. review transcribed letters for meaning rather than for errors in typing or transcription
    D. review transcribed letters for errors in typing rather than for errors in transcription

23. In transcribing a letter, the secretary notes that the dictator said, "The series of conferences are planned to be relevant to today's problems." In such a case, the secretary should
    A. type the sentence as it appears in the notes
    B. check with the dictator to see whether he would prefer a different grammatical construction
    C. change the noun so that it is correct
    D. revise the sentence as much as necessary to make it read better

24. Of the following, the BEST procedure for your staff to follow in transcribing several letters that were dictated is to
    A. transcribe first the letters that are most difficult so that they can return immediately to the dictator with any questions
    B. read through the notes for each letter to be sure they have all the information needed before preparing the transcript
    C. transcribe first those letters that are shortest and simplest in order to get them out of the way
    D. read all the notes aloud to a co-worker to see whether they sound right

25. In typing long letters, which of the following is generally considered the LEAST desirable practice?
    A. Numbering the second and succeeding pages of the letter
    B. Typing a single line of a new paragraph as the last line of a page
    C. Dividing a word at the end of a line of typing
    D. Typing the name of the recipient of the letter on the second and succeeding pages

KEY (CORRECT ANSWERS)

1.	C	11.	D
2.	D	12.	B
3.	D	13.	A
4.	B	14.	C
5.	C	15.	D
6.	A	16.	A
7.	D	17.	A
8.	A	18.	A
9.	B	19.	B
10.	C	20.	C

21. C
22. B
23. B
24. B
25. B

TEST 2

DIRECTIONS: Each question or incomplete statement is followed by several suggested answers or completions. Select the one that BEST answers the question or completes the statement. *PRINT THE LETTER OF THE CORRECT ANSWER IN THE SPACE AT THE RIGHT.*

1. The use of a microfilm system for information storage and retrieval would make the MOST sense in an office where
    A. a great number of documents must be kept available for permanent reference
    B. documents are ordinarily kept on file for less than six months
    C. filing is a minor and unimportant part of the office work
    D. most of the records on file are working forms on which additional entries are frequently made

    1.____

2. Of the following concepts, the one which CANNOT be represented suitably by a pie chart is
    A. percent shares
    B. shares in absolute units
    C. time trends
    D. successive totals over time, with their shares

    2.____

3. A pictogram is ESSENTIALLY another version of a(n) _____ chart.
    A. plain bar   B. component bar
    C. pie   D. area

    3.____

4. A time series for a certain cost is presented in a graph. It is drawn so that the vertical (cost) axis starts at a point well above zero. This is a legitimate method of presentation for some purposes, but it may have the effect of
    A. hiding fixed components of the cost
    B. exaggerating changes which, in actual amounts, may be insignificant
    C. minimizing variable components of the cost
    D. impairing correlation analysis

    4.____

5. Certain budgetary data may be represented by bar, area, or volume charts. Which one of the following BEST expressed the most appropriate order of usefulness?
    A. Descends from bar to volume and area charts, the last two being about the same
    B. Descends from volume to area, to bar charts
    C. Depends on the nature of the data presented
    D. Descends from bar to area to volume charts

    5.____

6. One weekend, you develop a painful infection in one hand. You know that your typing speed will be much slower than normal and the likelihood of your making mistakes will be increased.
   Of the following, the BEST course of action for you to take in this situation is to
   A. report to work as scheduled and do your typing assignments as best you can without complaining
   B. report to work as scheduled and ask your co-workers to divide your typing assignments until your hand heals
   C. report to work as scheduled and ask your supervisor for non-typing assignments until your hand heals
   D. call in sick and remain on medical leave until your hand is completely healed so that you can perform your normal duties

7. When filling out a departmental form during an interview concerning a citizen complaint, an interviewer should know the purpose of each question that he asks the citizen. For such information to be supplied by your department is
   A. *advisable*, because the interviewer may lose interest in the job if he is not fully informed about the questions he has to ask
   B. *inadvisable*, because the interviewer may reveal the true purpose of the questions to the citizens
   C. *advisable*, because the interviewer might otherwise record superficial or inadequate answers if he does not fully understand the questions
   D. *inadvisable*, because the information obtained through the form may be of little importance to the interviewer

8. The one of the following which is the BEST reason for placing the date and time of receipt on incoming mail is that this procedure
   A. aids the filing of correspondence in alphabetical order
   B. fixes responsibility for promptness in answering correspondence
   C. indicates that the mail has been checked for the presence of a return address
   D. makes it easier to distribute the main in sequence

9. Which one of the following is the FIRST step that you should take when filing a document by subject?
   A. Arrange related documents by date with the latest date in front
   B. Check whether the document has been released for filing
   C. Cross-reference the document if necessary
   D. Determine the category under which the document will be filed

10. The one of the following which is NOT generally employed to keep track of frequently used material requiring future attention is a
    A. card tickler file   B. dated follow-up folder
    C. periodic transferal of records   D. signal folder

11. Which one of the following is NOT a useful filing practice?
    A. Filing active records in the most accessible parts of the file cabinet
    B. Filing a file drawer to capacity in order to save space
    C. Gluing small documents to standard-size paper before filing
    D. Using different colored labels for various filing categories

12. The one of the following cases in which you would NOT place a special notation in the left margin of a letter that you have typed is when
    A. one of the copies is intended for someone other than the addressee of the letter
    B. you enclose a flyer with the letter
    C. you sign your superior's name to the letter, at his or her request
    D. the letter refers to something being sent under separate cover

13. Suppose that you accidentally cut a letter or enclosure as you are opening an envelope with a paper knife. The one of the following that you should do FIRST is to
    A. determine whether the document is important
    B. clip or staple the pieces together and process as usual
    C. mend the cut document with transparent tape
    D. notify the sender that the communication was damaged and request another copy

14. It is generally advisable to leave at least six inches of working space in a file drawer. This procedure is MOST useful in
    A. decreasing the number of filing errors
    B. facilitating the sorting of documents and folders
    C. maintaining a regular program of removing inactive records
    D. preventing folders and papers from being torn

15. Of the following, the MOST important reason to sort large volumes of documents before filing is that sorting
    A. decreases the need for cross-referencing
    B. eliminates the need to keep the filing up-to-date
    C. prevents overcrowding of the file drawers
    D. saves time and energy in filing

16. When typing a preliminary draft of a report, the one of the following which you should generally NOT do is to
    A. erase typing errors and deletions rather than "X"ing them out
    B. leave plenty of room at the top, bottom, and sides of each page
    C. make only the number of copies that you are asked to make
    D. type double or triple space

17. When printing a 500-page office manual, the most efficient method is to use which of the following office machines?   17._____
    A. Inkjet printer
    B. Copy machine
    C. Word processor
    D. All-in-one scanner/fax/copier

18. When typing name or titles on a roll of folder labels, the one of the following which it is MOST important to do is to type the caption   18._____
    A. as it appears son the papers to be placed in the folder
    B. in capital letters
    C. in exact indexing or filing order
    D. so that it appears near the bottom of the folder tab when the label is attached

19. The MOST important reason for having color cartridges on hand for an office copier even though most prints are black and white is because   19._____
    A. color ink is used for all copies
    B. some copiers or printers will not print black and white if any of the color cartridges are empty
    C. black ink is cheaper when purchasing along with color cartridges
    D. lack of color ink can cause copier malfunctions

20. All of the following pertain to the formatting of word-processing documents EXCEPT   20._____
    A. headers and footers
    B. rows and columns
    C. indents and page breaks
    D. alignment and justified type

KEY (CORRECT ANSWERS)

1.	A	11.	B
2.	C	12.	C
3.	A	13.	C
4.	B	14.	D
5.	D	15.	D
6.	C	16.	A
7.	C	17.	B
8.	B	18.	C
9.	B	19.	B
10.	C	20.	B

PREPARING WRITTEN MATERIAL

PARAGRAPH REARRANGEMENT
COMMENTARY

The sentences that follow are in scrambled order. You are to rearrange them in proper order and indicate the letter choice containing the correct answer at the space at the right.

Each group of sentences in this section is actually a paragraph presented in scrambled order. Each sentence in the group has a place in that paragraph; no sentence is to be left out. You are to read each group of sentences and decide upon the best order in which to put the sentences so as to form a well-organized paragraph.

The questions in this section measure the ability to solve a problem when all the facts relevant to its solution are not given.

More specifically, certain positions of responsibility and authority require the employee to discover connection between events sometimes, apparently, unrelated. In order to do this, the employee will find it necessary to correctly infer that unspecified events have probably occurred or are likely to occur. This ability becomes especially important when action must be taken on incomplete information.

Accordingly, these questions require competitors to choose among several suggested alternatives, each of which presents a different sequential arrangement of the events. Competitors must choose the MOST logical of the suggested sequences.

In order to do so, they may be required to draw on general knowledge to infer missing concepts or events that are essential to sequencing the given events. Competitors should be careful to infer only what is essential to the sequence. The plausibility of the wrong alternatives will always require the inclusion of unlikely events or of additional chains of events which are NOT essential to sequencing the given events.

It's very important to remember that you are looking for the best of the four possible choices, and that the best choice of all may not even be one of the answers you're given to choose from.

There is no one right way to solve these problems. Many people have found it helpful to first write out the order of the sentences, as they would have arranged them, on their scrap paper before looking at the possible answers. If their optimum answer is there, this can save them some time. If it isn't, this method can still give insight into solving the problem. Others find it most helpful to just go through each of the possible choices, contrasting each as they go along. You should use whatever method feels comfortable and works for you.

While most of these types of questions are not that difficult, we've added a higher percentage of the difficult type, just to give you more practice. Usually there are only one or two questions on this section that contain such subtle distinctions that you're unable to answer confidently. And you then may find yourself stuck deciding between two possible choices, neither of which you're sure about.

EXAMINATION SECTION

TEST 1

DIRECTIONS: The sentences that follow are in scrambled order. You are to rearrange them in proper order and indicate the letter choice containing the correct answer. *PRINT THE LETTER OF THE CORRECT ANSWER IN THE SPACE AT THE RIGHT.*

1. Below are four statements labeled W, X, Y and Z.
   W. He was a strict and fanatic drillmaster.
   X. The word is always used in a derogatory sense and generally shows resentment and anger on the part of the user.
   Y. It is from the name of this Frenchman that we derive our English word, martinet.
   Z. Jean Martinet was the Inspector-General of Infantry during the reign of King Louis XIV.
   The PROPER order in which these sentences should be placed in a paragraph is:
   A. X, Z, W, Y   B. X, Z, Y, W   C. Z, W, Y, X   D. Z, Y, W, X

   1.____

2. In the following paragraph, the sentences, which are numbered, have been jumbled.
   I. Since then it has undergone changes.
   II. It was incorporated in 1955 under the laws of the State of New York.
   III. Its primary purposes, a cleaner city, has, however, remained the same.
   IV. The Citizens Committee works in cooperation with the Mayor's Inter-departmental Committee for a Clean City.
   The order in which these sentences should be arranged to form a well-organized paragraph is:
   A. II, IV, I, III   B. III, IV, I, II   C. IV, II, I, III   D. IV, III, II, I

   2.____

   3.____

Questions 3-5.

DIRECTIONS: The sentences listed below are part of a meaningful paragraph but they are not given in their proper order. You are to decide what would be the BEST order in which to put the sentences so as to form a well-organized paragraph. Each sentence has a place in the paragraph; there are no extra sentences. You are then to answer Questions 3 through 5 inclusive on the basis of your rearrangements of these scrambled sentences into a properly organized paragraph.

In 1887 some insurance companies organized an Inspection Department to advise their clients on all phases of fire prevention and protection. Probably this has been due to the smaller annual fire losses in Great Britain than in the United States. It tests various fire prevention devices and appliances and determines manufacturing hazards and their safeguards. Fire research began earlier in the United States and is more advanced than in Great Britain. Later they established a laboratory specializing in electrical, mechanical, hydraulic, and chemical fields.

115

3. When the five sentences are arranged in proper order, the paragraph starts with the sentence which begins
   A. "In 1887..."   B. "Probably this..."   C. "It tests..."
   D. "Fire research..."   E. "Later they..."

4. In the last sentence listed above, "they" refers to
   A. the insurance companies   B. the United States and Great Britain
   C. the Inspection Department   D. clients
   E. technicians

5. When the above paragraph is properly arranged, it ends with the words
   A. "...and protection."   B. "...the United States."
   C. "...their safeguards."   D. "...in Great Britain."
   E. "...chemical fields."

KEY (CORRECT ANSWERS)

1. C
2. C
3. D
4. A
5. C

TEST 2

DIRECTIONS: In each of the questions numbered I through V, several sentences are given. For each question, choose as your answer the group of number that represents the MOST logical order of these sentences if they were arranged in paragraph form. *PRINT THE LETTER OF THE CORRECT ANSWER IN THE SPACE AT THE RIGHT.*

1.   I. It is established when one shows that the landlord has prevented the tenant's enjoyment of his interest in the property leased.
    II. Constructive eviction is the result of a breach of the covenant of quiet enjoyment implied in all leases.
    III. In some parts of the United States, it is not complete until the tenant vacates within a reasonable time.
    IV. Generally, the acts must be of such serious and permanent character as to deny the tenant the enjoyment of his possessing rights.
    V. In this event, upon abandonment of the premises, the tenant's liability for that ceases.
    The CORRECT answer is:
    A. II, I, IV, III, V
    B. V, II, III, I, IV
    C. IV, III, I, II, V
    D. I, III, V, IV, II

1.____

2.   I. The powerlessness before private and public authorities that is the typical experience of the slum tenant is reminiscent of the situation of blue-collar workers all through the nineteenth century.
    II. Similarly, in recent years, this chapter of history has been reopened by anti-poverty groups which have attempted to organize slum tenants to enable them to bargain collectively with their landlords about the conditions of their tenancies.
    III. It is familiar history that many of the worker remedied their condition by joining together and presenting their demands collectively.
    IV. Like the workers, tenants are forced by the conditions of modern life into substantial dependence on these who possess great political aid and economic power.
    V. What's more, the very fact of dependence coupled with an absence of education and self-confidence makes them hesitant and unable to stand up for what they need from those in power.
    The CORRECT answer is:
    A. V, IV, I, II, III
    B. II, III, I, V, IV
    C. III, I, V, IV, II
    D. I, IV, V, III, II

2.____

3.   I. A railroad, for example, when not acting as a common carrier may contract away responsibility for its own negligence.
    II. As to a landlord, however, no decision has been found relating to the legal effect of a clause shifting the statutory duty of repair to the tenant.
    III. The courts have not passed on the validity of clauses relieving the landlord of this duty and liability.
    IV. They have, however, upheld the validity of exculpatory clauses in other types of contracts.

3.____

117

V. Housing regulations impose a duty upon the landlord to maintain leased premises in safe condition.
VI. As another example, a bailee may limit his liability except for gross negligence, willful acts, or fraud.

The CORRECT answer is:
A. II, I, VI, IV, III, V
B. I, III, IV, V, VI, II
C. III, V, I, IV, II, VI
D. V, III, IV, I, VI, II

4.
I. Since there are only samples in the building, retail or consumer sales are generally eschewed by mart occupants, and in some instances, rigid controls are maintained to limit entrance to the mart only to those persons engaged in retailing.
II. Since World War I, in many larger cities, there has developed a new type of property, called the mart building.
III. It can, therefore, be used by wholesalers and jobbers for the display of sample merchandise.
IV. This type of building is most frequently a multi-storied, finished interior property which is a cross between a retail arcade and a loft building.
V. This limitation enables the mart occupants to ship the orders from another location after the retailer or dealer makes his selection from the samples.

The CORRECT answer is:
A. II, IV, III, I, V
B. IV, III, V, I, II
C. I, III, II, IV, V
D. I, IV, II, III, V

5.
I. In general, staff-line friction reduces the distinctive contribution of staff personnel.
II. The conflicts, however, introduce an uncontrolled element into the managerial system.
III. On the other hand, the natural resistance of the line to staff innovations probably usefully restrains over-eager efforts to apply untested procedures on a large scale.
IV. Under such conditions, it is difficult to know when valuable ideas are being sacrificed.
V. The relatively weak position of staff, requiring accommodation to the line, tends to restrict their ability to engage in free, experimental innovation.

The CORRECT answer is:
A. IV, II, III, I, V
B. I, V, III, II, IV
C. V, III, I, II, IV
D. II, I, IV, V, III

KEY (CORRECT ANSWERS)

1. A
2. D
3. D
4. A
5. B

TEST 3

DIRECTIONS: Questions 1 through 4 consist of six sentences which can be arranged in a logical sequence. For each question, select the choice which places the numbered sentences in the MOST logical sequent. *PRINT THE LETTER OF THE CORRECT ANSWER IN THE SPACE AT THE RIGHT.*

1. I. The burden of proof as to each issue is determined before trial and remains upon the same party throughout the trial.
    II. The jury is at liberty to believe one witness' testimony as against a number of contradictory witnesses.
    III. In a civil case, the party bearing the burden of proof is required to prove his contention by a fair preponderance of the evidence.
    IV. However, it must be noted that a fair preponderance of evidence does not necessarily mean a greater number of witnesses.
    V. The burden of proof is the burden which rests upon one of the parties to an action to persuade the trier of the facts, generally the jury, that a proposition he asserts is true.
    VI. If the evidence is equally balanced, or if it leaves the jury in such doubt as to be unable to decide the controversy either way, judgment must be given against the party upon whom the burden of proof rests.
    The CORRECT answer is:
    A. III, II, V, IV, I, VI
    B. I, II, VI, V, III, IV
    C. III, IV, V, I, II, VI
    D. V, I, III, VI, IV, II

    1.____

2. I. If a parent is without assets and is unemployed, he cannot be convicted of the crime of non-support of a child.
    II. The term "sufficient ability" has been held to mean sufficient financial ability.
    III. It does not matter if his unemployment is by choice or unavoidable circumstances.
    IV. If he fails to take any steps at all, he may be liable to prosecution for endangering the welfare of a child.
    V. Under the penal law, a parent is responsible for the support of his minor child only if the parent is "of sufficient ability."
    VI. An indigent parent may meet his obligation by borrowing money or by seeking aid under the provisions of the Social Welfare Law.
    The CORRECT answer is:
    A. VI, I, V, III, II, IV
    B. I, III, V, II, IV, VI
    C. V, II, I, III, VI, IV
    D. I, VI, IV, V, II, III

    2.____

3. I. Consider, for example, the case of a rabble rouser who urges a group of twenty people to go out and break the windows of a nearby factory.
    II. Therefore, the law fills the indicated gap with the crime of inciting to riot.
    III. A person is considered guilty of inciting to riot when he urges ten or more persons to engage in tumultuous and violent conduct of a kind likely to create public alarm.
    IV. However, if he has not obtained the cooperation of at least four people, he cannot be charged with unlawful assembly.

    3.____

119

2 (#3)

- V. The charge of inciting to riot was added to the law to cover types of conduct which cannot be classified as either the crime of "riot" or the crime of "unlawful assembly."
- VI. If he acquires the acquiescence of at least four of them, he is guilty of unlawful assembly even if the project does not materialize.

The CORRECT answer is:
- A. III, V, I, VI, IV, II
- B. V, I, IV, VI, II, III
- C. III, IV, I, V, II, VI
- D. V, I, IV, VI, III, II

4.
- I. If, however, the rebuttal evidence presents an issue of credibility, it is for the jury to determine whether the presumption has, in fact, been destroyed.
- II. Once sufficient evidence to the contrary is introduced, the presumption disappears from the trial.
- III. The effect of a presumption is to place the burden upon the adversary to come forward with evidence to rebut the presumption.
- IV. When a presumption is overcome and ceases to exist in the case, the fact or facts which gave rise to the presumption still remain.
- V. Whether a presumption has been overcome is ordinarily a question for the court.
- VI. Such information may furnish a basis for a logical inference.

The CORRECT answer is:
- A. IV, VI, II, V, I, III
- B. III, II, V, I, IV, VI
- C. V, III, VI, IV, II, I
- D. V, IV, I, II, VI, III

4.____

KEY (CORRECT ANSWERS)

1. D
2. C
3. A
4. B

CODING

COMMENTARY

An ingenious question-type called coding, involving elements of alphabetizing, filing, name and number comparison, and evaluative judgment and application, has currently won wide acceptance in testing circles for measuring clerical aptitude and general ability, particularly on the senior (middle) grades (levels).

While the directions for this question-type usually vary in detail, the candidate is generally asked to consider groups of names, codes, and numbers, and, then, according to a given plan, to arrange codes in alphabetic order; to arrange these in numerical sequence; to rearrange columns of names and numbers in correct order; to espy errors in coding; to choose the correct coding arrangement in consonance with the given directions and examples, etc.

This question-type appears to have few parameters in respect to form, substance, or degree of difficulty.

Accordingly, acquaintance with, and practice in the coding question is recommended for the serious candidate.

EXAMINATION SECTION
TEST 1

DIRECTIONS: Questions 1 through 10 are to be answered on the basis of the following Code Table. In this table every letter has a corresponding code number to be punched. Each question contains three lines of letters and code numbers. In each line, the code numbers should correspond with the letters in accordance with the table.

Letter	M	X	R	T	W	A	E	Q	Z	C
Code	1	2	3	4	5	6	7	8	9	0

On some of the lines, an error exists in the coding. Compare the letters and numbers in each question carefully. If you find an error or errors on
    only *one* of the lines in the question, mark your answer A;
    any *two* lines in the question, mark your answer B;
    all *three* lines in the question, mark your answer C;
    none of the lines in the question, mark your answer D.

SAMPLE QUESTION

XAQMZMRQ	-	26819138
RAERQEX	-	3573872
TMZCMTZA	-	46901496

In the above sample, the first line is correct since each letter, as listed, has the correct corresponding code number.
In the second line, an error exists because the letter A should have the code number 6 instead of 5.
In the third line, an error exists because the letter W should have the code number 5 instead of 6.
Since there are errors in two of the three lines, your answer should be B.

1. EQRMATTR - 78316443
   MACWXRQW - 16052385
   XZEMCAR - 2971063

2. CZEMRXQ - 0971238
   XMTARET - 2146374
   WCEARWEC - 50863570

3. CEXAWRQZ - 07265389
   RCRMMZQT - 33011984
   ACMZWTEX - 60195472

4. XRCZQZWR - 23089953
   CMRQCAET - 01389574
   ZXRWTECM - 92345701

2 (#1)

5.	AXMTRAWR	-	62134653		5.____
	EQQCZCEW	-	77809075		
	MAZQARTM	-	16086341		
6.	WRWQCTRM	-	53580431		6.____
	CXMWAERZ	-	02156739		
	RCQEWWME	-	30865517		
7.	CRMECEAX	-	03170762		7.____
	MZCTRXRQ	-	19043238		
	XXZREMEW	-	22937175		
8.	MRCXQEAX	-	13928762		8.____
	WAMZTRMZ	-	65194319		
	ECXARWXC	-	70263520		
9.	MAWXECRQ	-	16527038		9.____
	RXQEAETM	-	32876741		
	RXEWMCZQ	-	32751098		
10.	MRQZCATE	-	13890647		10.____
	WCETRXAW	-	50743625		
	CZWMCERT	-	09510734		

KEY (CORRECT ANSWERS)

1. D
2. B
3. A
4. C
5. C

6. A
7. D
8. B
9. D
10. A

TEST 2

DIRECTIONS: Questions 1 through 6 consist of three lines of code letters and numbers. The numbers on each, line should correspond with the code letters on the same line in accordance with the table below.

Code Letter	F	X	L	M	R	W	T	S	B	H
Corresponding Number	0	1	2	3	4	5	6	7	8	9

On some of the lines, an error exists in the coding. Compare the letters and numbers in each question carefully. If you find an error or errors on
  only *one* of the lines in the question, mark your answer A;
  any *two* lines in the question, mark your answer B;
  all *three* lines in the question, mark your answer C;
  none of the lines in the question, mark your answer D.

SAMPLE QUESTION

  LTSXHMF   2671930
  TBRWHLM   6845913
  SXLBFMR   5128034

In the above sample, the first line is correct since each code letter listed has the correct corresponding number.
  On the second line, an error exists because code letter L should have the number 2 instead of the number 1.
  On the third line, an error exists because the code letter S should have the number 7 instead of the number 5.
  Since there are errors on two of the three lines, the correct answer is B.

1. XMWBHLR   1358924
   FWSLRHX   0572491
   MTXBLTS   3618267

   1.____

2. XTLSMRF   1627340
   BMHRFLT   8394026
   HLTSWRX   9267451

   2.____

3. LMBSFXS   2387016
   RWLMBSX   4532871
   SMFXBHW   7301894

   3.____

4. RSTWTSML   47657632
   LXRMHFBS   21439087
   FTLBMRWX   06273451

   4.____

5. XSRSBWFM   17478603
   BRMXRMXT   84314216
   XSTFBWRL   17609542

   5.____

124

6. TMSBXHLS 63781927
   RBSFLFWM 48702053
   MHFXWTRS 39015647

6.____

KEY (CORRECT ANSWERS)

1. D
2. A
3. C
4. B
5. C
6. D

TEST 3

DIRECTIONS: Questions 1 through 5 consist of three lines of code letters and numbers. The numbers on each line should correspond with the code letters on the same line in accordance with the table below.

Code Letter	P	L	I	J	B	O	H	U	C	G
Corresponding Number	0	1	2	3	4	5	6	7	8	9

On some of the lines, an error exists in the coding. Compare the letters and numbers in each question carefully. If you find an error or errors on
 only *one* of the lines in the question, mark your answer A;
 any *two* lines in the question, mark your answer B;
 all *three* lines in the question, mark your answer C;
 none of the lines in the question, mark your answer D.

SAMPLE QUESTION

JHOILCP 3652180
BICLGUP 4286970
UCIBHLJ 5824613

In the above sample, the first line is correct since each code letter listed has the correct corresponding number.
On the second line, an error exists because code letter L should have the number 1 instead of the number 6.
On the third line an error exists because the code letter U should have the number 7 instead of the number 5.
Since there are errors on two of the three lines, the correct answer is B.

1. BULJCIP 4713920
   HIGPOUL 6290571
   OCUHJBI 5876342

2. CUBLOIJ 8741023
   LCLGCLB 1818914
   JPUHIOC 3076158

3. OIJGCBPO 52398405
   UHPBLIOP 76041250
   CLUIPGPC 81720908

4. BPCOUOJI 40875732
   UOHCIPLB 75682014
   GLHUUCBJ 92677843

5. HOIOHJLH 65256361
   IOJJHHBP 25536640
   OJHBJOPI 53642502

KEY (CORRECT ANSWERS)

1. A
2. C
3. D
4. B
5. C

TEST 4

DIRECTIONS: Questions 1 through 5 consist of three lines of code letters and numbers. The numbers on each line should correspond with the code letters on the same line in accordance with the table below.

Code Letters	Q	S	L	Y	M	O	U	N	W	Z
Corresponding Numbers	1	2	3	4	5	6	7	8	9	0

On some of the lines, an error exists in the coding. Compare the letters and numbers in each question carefully. If you find an error on

only *one* of the lines in the question, mark your answer A;
any *two* lines in the question, mark your answer B;
all *three* lines in the question, mark your answer C;
none of the lines in the question, mark your answer D.

SAMPLE QUESTION
MOQNWZQS   56189012
QWNMOLYU   19865347
LONLMYWN   36835489

In the above sample, the first line is correct since each code letter, as listed, has the correct corresponding number.
On the second line, an error exists because code letter M should have the number 5 instead of the number 6.
On the third line an error exists because the code letter W should have the number 9 instead of the number 8.
Since there are errors on two of the three lines, the correct answer is B.

1. SMUWOLQN   25796318
    ULSQNMZL   73218503
    NMYQZUSL   85410723

2. YUWWMYQZ   47995410
    SOSOSQSO   26262126
    ZUNLWMYW   07839549

3. QULSWZYN   17329045
    ZYLQWOYF   04319639
    QLUYWZSO   13749026

4. NLQZOYUM   83106475
    SQMUWZOM   21579065
    MMYWMZSQ   55498021

5. NQLOWZZU   81319007
    SMYLUNZO   25347806
    UWMSNZOL   79528013

1.____

2.____

3.____

4.____

5.____

128

KEY (CORRECT ANSWERS)

1. D
2. D
3. B
4. A
5. C

TEST 5

DIRECTIONS: Answer Questions 1 through 6 *SOLELY* on the basis of the chart and the instructions given below.

Toll Rate	$.25	$.30	$.45	$.60	$.75	$8.90	$1.20	$2.50
Classification Number of Vehicle	1	2	3	4	5	6	7	8

Assume that each of the amounts of money on the above chart is a toll rate charged for a type of vehicle and that the number immediately below each amount is the classification number for that type of vehicle. For instance, "1" is the classification number for a vehicle paying a $.25 toll; "2" is the classification number for a vehicle paying a $.30 toll; and so forth.

In each question, a series of tolls is given in Column I. Column II gives four different arrangements of classification numbers. You are to pick the answer (A, B, C, or D) in Column II that gives the classification numbers that match the tolls in Column I and are in the same order as the tolls in Column I.

SAMPLE QUESTION

Column I	Column II
$.30, $.90, $2.50, $.45	A. 2, 6, 8, 2
	B. 2, 8, 6, 3
	C. 2, 6, 8, 3
	D. 1, 6, 8, 3

According to the chart, the classification numbers that correspond to these toll rates are as follows: $.30 - 2, $.90 - 6, $2.50 - 8, $.45 -3. Therefore, the right answer is 2, 6, 8, 3. The answer is C in Column II.

Do the following questions in the same way.

Column I   Column II

1. $.60, $.30, $.90, $1.20, $.60
   A. 4, 6, 2, 8, 4
   B. 4, 2, 6, 7, 4
   C. 2, 4, 7, 6, 2
   D. 2, 4, 6, 7, 4

   1.____

2. $.90, $.45, $.25, $.45, $2.50, $.75
   A. 6, 3, 1, 3, 8, 3
   B. 6, 3, 3, 1, 8, 5
   C. 6, 1, 3, 3, 8, 5
   D. 6, 3, 1, 3, 8, 5

   2.____

3. $.45, $.75, $1.20, $.25, $.25, $.30, $.45
   A. 3, 5, 7, 1, 1, 2, 3
   B. 5, 3, 7, 1, 1, 2, 3
   C. 3, 5, 7, 1, 2, 1, 3
   D. 3, 7, 5, 1, 1, 2, 3

   3.____

4. $1.20, $2.50, $.45, $.90, $1.20, $.75, $.25
   A. 7, 8, 5, 6, 7, 5, 1
   B. 7, 8, 3, 7, 6, 5, 1
   C. 7, 8, 3, 6, 7, 5, 1
   D. 7, 8, 3, 6, 7, 1, 5

   4.____

2 (#5)

5. $2.50, $1.20, $.90, $.25, $.60, $.45, $.30
    A. 8, 6, 7, 1, 4, 3, 2
    B. 8, 7, 5, 1, 4, 3, 2
    C. 8, 7, 6, 2, 4, 3, 2
    D. 8, 7, 6, 1, 4, 3, 2

5.____

6. $.75, $.25, $.45, $.60, $.90, $.30, $2.50
    A. 5, 1, 3, 2, 4, 6, 8
    B. 5, 1, 3, 4, 2, 6, 8
    C. 5, 1, 3, 4, 6, 2, 8
    D. 5, 3, 1, 4, 6, 2, 8

6.____

KEY (CORRECT ANSWERS)

1. B
2. D
3. A
4. C
5. D
6. C

TEST 6

DIRECTIONS: Answer Questions 1 through 10 on the basis of the following information:
A code number for any item is obtained by combining the date of delivery, number of units received, and number of units used. The first two digits represent the day of the month, the third and fourth digits represent the month, and the fifth and sixth digits represent the year.
The number following the letter R represents the number of units received and the number following the letter U represents the number of units used.
For example, the code number 120603-R5690-U1001 indicates that a delivery of 5,690 units was made on June 12, 2003 of which 1,001 units were used.

Questions 1-6.

DIRECTIONS: Using the chart below, answer Questions 1 through 6 by choosing the letter (A, B, C, or D) in which the supplier and stock number correspond to the code number given.

Supplier	Stock Number	Number of Units Received	Delivery Date	Number of Units Used
Stony	38390	8300	May 11, 2002	3800
Stoney	39803	1780	September 15, 2003	1703
Nievo	21220	5527	October 10, 2003	5007
Nieve	38903	1733	August 5, 2003	1703
Monte	39213	5527	October 10, 2002	5007
Stony	38890	3308	December 9, 2002	3300
Stony	83930	3880	September 12, 2002	380
Nevo	47101	485	June 11, 2002	231
Nievo	12122	5725	May 11, 2003	5201
Neve	47101	9721	August 15, 2003	8207
Nievo	21120	2275	January 7, 2002	2175
Rosa	41210	3821	March 3, 2003	2710
Stony	38890	3308	September 12, 2002	3300
Dinal	54921	1711	April 2, 2003	1117
Stony	33890	8038	March 5, 2003	3300
Dinal	54721	1171	March 2, 2002	717
Claridge	81927	3308	April 5, 2003	3088
Nievo	21122	4878	June 7, 2002	3492
Haley	39670	8300	December 23, 2003	5300

1. Code No. 120902-R3308-U3300

   A. Nievo - 12122   B. Stony - 83930
   C. Nievo - 21220   D. Stony - 38890

2. Code No. 101002-R5527-U5007

   A. Nievo - 21220   B. Haley - 39670
   C. Monte - 39213   D. Claridge - 81927

3. Code No. 101003-R5527-U5007

   A. Nievo - 21220   B. Monte - 39213
   C. Nievo - 12122   D. Nievo - 21120

4. Code No. 110503-R5725-U5201   4._____

   A. Nievo - 12122   B. Nievo - 21220
   C. Haley - 39670   D. Stony - 38390

5. Code No. 070102-R2275-U2175   5._____

   A. Stony - 33890   B. Stony - 83930
   C. Stony - 38390   D. Nievo - 21120

6. Code No. 120902-R3880-U380   6._____

   A. Stony - 83930   B. Stony - 38890
   C. Stony - 33890   D. Monte - 39213

Questions 7-10.

DIRECTIONS: Using the same chart, answer Questions 7 through 10 by choosing the letter (A, B, C, or D) in which the code number corresponds to the supplier and stock number given.

7. Nieve - 38903   7._____

   A. 851903-R1733-U1703   B. 080502-R1733-U1703
   C. 080503-R1733-U1703   D. 050803-R1733-U1703

8. Nevo - 47101   8._____

   A. 081503-R9721-U8207   B. 091503-R9721-U8207
   C. 110602-R485-U231   D. 061102-R485-U231

9. Dinal - 54921   9._____

   A. 020403-R1711-U1117   B. 030202-R1171-U717
   C. 020302-R1171-U717   D. 421903-R1711-U1117

10. Nievo - 21122   10._____

    A. 070602-R4878-U3492   B. 060702-R4878-U349
    C. 761902-R4878-U3492   D. 060702-R4878-U3492

KEY (CORRECT ANSWERS)

1. D
2. C
3. A
4. A
5. D

6. A
7. D
8. C
9. A
10. A

PHILOSOPHY, PRINCIPLES, PRACTICES, AND TECHNICS
OF
SUPERVISION, ADMINISTRATION, MANAGEMENT, AND ORGANIZATION

TABLE OF CONTENTS

	Page
MEANING OF SUPERVISION	1
THE OLD AND THE NEW SUPERVISION	1
THE EIGHT (8) BASIC PRINCIPLES OF THE NEW SUPERVISION	1
I. Principle of Responsibility	1
II. Principle of Authority	2
III. Principle of Self-Growth	2
IV. Principle of Individual Worth	2
V. Principle of Creative Leadership	2
VI. Principle of Success and Failure	2
VII. Principle of Science	3
VIII. Principle of Cooperation	3
WHAT IS ADMINISTRATION?	3
I. Practices Commonly Classed as "Supervisory"	3
II. Practices Commonly Classed as "Administrative"	3
III. Practices Commonly Classed as Both "Supervisory" and "Administrative"	4
RESPONSIBILITIES OF THE SUPERVISOR	4
COMPETENCIES OF THE SUPERVISOR	4
THE PROFESSIONAL SUPERVISOR-EMPLOYEE RELATIONSHIP	4
MINI-TEXT IN SUPERVISION, ADMINISTRATION, MANAGEMENT, AND ORGANIZATION	5
I. Brief Highlights	5
A. Levels of Management	6
B. What the Supervisor Must Learn	6
C. A Definition of Supervision	6
D. Elements of the Team Concept	6
E. Principles of Organization	6
F. The Four Important Parts of Every Job	7
G. Principles of Delegation	7
H. Principles of Effective Communications	7
I. Principles of Work Improvement	7
J. Areas of Job Improvement	7
K. Seven Key Points in Making Improvements	8

L.	Corrective Techniques for Job Improvement	8
M.	A Planning Checklist	8
N.	Five Characteristics of Good Directions	9
O.	Types of Directions	9
P.	Controls	9
Q.	Orienting the New Employee	9
R.	Checklist for Orienting New Employees	9
S.	Principles of Learning	10
T.	Causes of Poor Performance	10
U.	Four Major Steps in On-the-Job Instructions	10
V.	Employees Want Five Things	10
W.	Some Don'ts in Regard to Praise	11
X.	How to Gain Your Workers' Confidence	11
Y.	Sources of Employee Problems	11
Z.	The Supervisor's Key to Discipline	11
AA.	Five Important Processes of Management	12
BB.	When the Supervisor Fails to Plan	12
CC.	Fourteen General Principles of Management	12
DD.	Change	12

II. Brief Topical Summaries — 13
- A. Who/What is the Supervisor? — 13
- B. The Sociology of Work — 13
- C. Principles and Practices of Supervision — 14
- D. Dynamic Leadership — 14
- E. Processes for Solving Problems — 15
- F. Training for Results — 15
- G. Health, Safety, and Accident Prevention — 16
- H. Equal Employment Opportunity — 16
- I. Improving Communications — 16
- J. Self-Development — 17
- K. Teaching and Training — 17
  1. The Teaching Process — 17
     a. Preparation — 17
     b. Presentation — 18
     c. Summary — 18
     d. Application — 18
     e. Evaluation — 18
  2. Teaching Methods — 18
     a. Lecture — 18
     b. Discussion — 18
     c. Demonstration — 19
     d. Performance — 19
     e. Which Method to Use — 19

PHILOSOPHY, PRINCIPLES, PRACTICES, AND TECHNICS
OF
SUPERVISION, ADMINISTRATION, MANAGEMENT, AND ORGANIZATION

MEANING OF SUPERVISION

The extension of the democratic philosophy has been accompanied by an extension in the scope of supervision. Modern leaders and supervisors no longer think of supervision in the narrow sense of being confined chiefly to visiting employees, supplying materials, or rating the staff. They regard supervision as being intimately related to all the concerned agencies of society, they speak of the supervisor's function in terms of "growth," rather than the "improvement" of employees.

This modern concept of supervision may be defined as follows: Supervision is leadership and the development of leadership within groups which are cooperatively engaged in inspection, research, training, guidance, and evaluation.

THE OLD AND THE NEW SUPERVISION

TRADITIONAL
1. Inspection
2. Focused on the employee
3. Visitation
4. Random and haphazard
5. Imposed and authoritarian
6. One person usually

MODERN
1. Study and analysis
2. Focused on aims, materials, methods, supervisors, employees, environment
3. Demonstrations, intervisitation, workshops, directed reading, bulletins, etc.
4. Definitely organized and planned (scientific)
5. Cooperative and democratic
6. Many persons involved (creative)

THE EIGHT (8) BASIC PRINCIPLES OF THE NEW SUPERVISION

I. Principle of Responsibility
   Authority to act and responsibility for acting must be joined.
   A. If you give responsibility, give authority.
   B. Define employee duties clearly.
   C. Protect employees from criticism by others.
   D. Recognize the rights as well as obligations of employees.
   E. Achieve the aims of a democratic society insofar as it is possible within the area of your work.
   F. Establish a situation favorable to training and learning.
   G. Accept ultimate responsibility for everything done in your section, unit, office, division, department.
   H. Good administration and good supervision are inseparable.

II. Principle of Authority
The success of the supervisor is measured by the extent to which the power of authority is not used.
   A. Exercise simplicity and informality in supervision
   B. Use the simplest machinery of supervision
   C. If it is good for the organization as a whole, it is probably justified.
   D. Seldom be arbitrary or authoritative.
   E. Do not base your work on the power of position or of personality.
   F. Permit and encourage the free expression of opinions.

III. Principle of Self-Growth
The success of the supervisor is measured by the extent to which, and the speed with which, he is no longer needed.
   A. Base criticism on principles, not on specifics.
   B. Point out higher activities to employees.
   C. Train for self-thinking by employees to meet new situations.
   D. Stimulate initiative, self-reliance, and individual responsibility
   E. Concentrate on stimulating the growth of employees rather than on removing defects.

IV. Principle of Individual Worth
Respect for the individual is a paramount consideration in supervision.
   A. Be human and sympathetic in dealing with employees.
   B. Don't nag about things to be done.
   C. Recognize the individual differences among employees and seek opportunities to permit best expression of each personality.

V. Principle of Creative Leadership
The best supervision is that which is not apparent to the employee.
   A. Stimulate, don't drive employees to creative action.
   B. Emphasize doing good things.
   C. Encourage employees to do what they do best.
   D. Do not be too greatly concerned with details of subject or method.
   E. Do not be concerned exclusively with immediate problems and activities.
   F. Reveal higher activities and make them both desired and maximally possible.
   G. Determine procedures in the light of each situation but see that these are derived from a sound basic philosophy.
   H. Aid, inspire, and lead so as to liberate the creative spirit latent in all good employees.

VI. Principle of Success and Failure
There are no unsuccessful employees, only unsuccessful supervisors who have failed to give proper leadership.
   A. Adapt suggestions to the capacities, attitudes, and prejudices of employees.
   B. Be gradual, be progressive, be persistent.
   C. Help the employee find the general principle; have the employee apply his own problem to the general principle.
   D. Give adequate appreciation for good work and honest effort.
   E. Anticipate employee difficulties and help to prevent them.
   F. Encourage employees to do the desirable things they will do anyway.
   G. Judge your supervision by the results it secures.

VII. Principle of Science
Successful supervision is scientific, objective, and experimental. It is based on facts, not on prejudices.
- A. Be cumulative in results.
- B. Never divorce your suggestions from the goals of training.
- C. Don't be impatient of results.
- D. Keep all matters on a professional, not a personal, level.
- E. Do not be concerned exclusively with immediate problems and activities.
- F. Use objective means of determining achievement and rating where possible.

VIII. Principle of Cooperation
Supervision is a cooperative enterprise between supervisor and employee.
- A. Begin with conditions as they are.
- B. Ask opinions of all involved when formulating policies.
- C. Organization is as good as its weakest link.
- D. Let employees help to determine policies and department programs.
- E. Be approachable and accessible—physically and mentally.
- F. Develop pleasant social relationships.

WHAT IS ADMINISTRATION

Administration is concerned with providing the environment, the material facilities, and the operational procedures that will promote the maximum growth and development of supervisors and employees. (Organization is an aspect and a concomitant of administration.)

There is no sharp line of demarcation between supervision and administration; these functions are intimately interrelated and, often, overlapping. They are complementary activities.

I. Practices Commonly Classed as "Supervisory"
- A. Conducting employees' conferences
- B. Visiting sections, units, offices, divisions, departments
- C. Arranging for demonstrations
- D. Examining plans
- E. Suggesting professional reading
- F. Interpreting bulletins
- G. Recommending in-service training courses
- H. Encouraging experimentation
- I. Appraising employee morale
- J. Providing for intervisitation

II. Practices Commonly Classified as "Administrative"
- A. Management of the office
- B. Arrangement of schedules for extra duties
- C. Assignment of rooms or areas
- D. Distribution of supplies
- E. Keeping records and reports
- F. Care of audio-visual materials
- G. Keeping inventory records
- H. Checking record cards and books

I. Programming special activities
J. Checking on the attendance and punctuality of employees

III. Practices Commonly Classified as Both "Supervisory" and "Administrative"
   A. Program construction
   B. Testing or evaluating outcomes
   C. Personnel accounting
   D. Ordering instructional materials

RESPONSIBILITIES OF THE SUPERVISOR

A person employed in a supervisory capacity must constantly be able to improve his own efficiency and ability. He represent the employer to the employees and only continuous self-examination can make him a capable supervisor.

Leadership and training are the supervisor's responsibility. An efficient working unit is one in which the employees work with the supervisor. It is his job to bring out the best in his employees. He must always be relaxed, courteous, and calm in his association with his employees. Their feelings are important, and a harsh attitude does not develop the most efficient employees.

COMPETENCES OF THE SUPERVISOR

I. Complete knowledge of the duties and responsibilities of his position.
II. To be able to organize a job, plan ahead, and carry through.
III. To have self-confidence and initiative.
IV. To be able to handle the unexpected situation and make quick decisions.
V. To be able to properly train subordinates in the positions they are best suited for.
VI. To be able to keep good human relations among his subordinates.
VII. To be able to keep good human relations between his subordinates and himself and to earn their respect and trust.

THE PROFESSIONAL SUPERVISOR-EMPLOYEE RELATIONSHIP

There are two kinds of efficiency: one kind is only apparent and is produced in organizations through the exercise of mere discipline; this is but a simulation of the second, or true, efficiency which springs from spontaneous cooperation. If you are a manager, no matter how great or small your responsibility, it is your job, in the final analysis, to create and develop this involuntary cooperation among the people whom you supervise. For, no matter how powerful a combination of money, machines, and materials a company may have, this is a dead and sterile thing without a team of willing, thinking, and articulate people to guide it.

The following 21 points are presented as indicative of the exemplary basic relationship that should exist between supervisor and employee:

1. Each person wants to be liked and respected by his fellow employee and wants to be treated with consideration and respect by his superior.
2. The most competent employee will make an error. However, in a unit where good relations exist between the supervisor and his employees, tenseness and fear do not exist. Thus, errors are not hidden or covered up, and the efficiency of a unit is not impaired.

3. Subordinates resent rules, regulations, or orders that are unreasonable or unexplained.
4. Subordinates are quick to resent unfairness, harshness, injustices, and favoritism.
5. An employee will accept responsibility if he knows that he will be complimented for a job well done, and not too harshly chastised for failure; that his supervisor will check the cause of the failure, and, if it was the supervisor's fault, he will assume the blame therefore. If it was the employee's fault, his supervisor will explain the correct method or means of handling the responsibility.
6. An employee wants to receive credit for a suggestion he has made, that is used. If a suggestion cannot be used, the employee is entitled to an explanation. The supervisor should not say "no" and close the subject.
7. Fear and worry slow up a worker's ability. Poor working environment can impair his physical and mental health. A good supervisor avoids forceful methods, threats, and arguments to get a job done.
8. A forceful supervisor is able to train his employees individually and as a team, and is able to motivate them in the proper channels.
9. A mature supervisor is able to properly evaluate his subordinates and to keep them happy and satisfied.
10. A sensitive supervisor will never patronize his subordinates.
11. A worthy supervisor will respect his employees' confidences.
12. Definite and clear-cut responsibilities should be assigned to each executive.
13. Responsibility should always be coupled with corresponding authority.
14. No change should be made in the scope or responsibilities of a position without a definite understanding to that effect on the part of all persons concerned.
15. No executive or employee, occupying a single position in the organization, should be subject to definite orders from more than one source.
16. Orders should never be given to subordinates over the head of a responsible executive. Rather than do this, the officer in question should be supplanted.
17. Criticisms of subordinates should, whoever possible, be made privately, and in no case should a subordinate be criticized in the presence of executives or employees of equal or lower rank.
18. No dispute or difference between executives or employees as to authority or responsibilities should be considered too trivial for prompt and careful adjudication.
19. Promotions, wage changes, and disciplinary action should always be approved by the executive immediately superior to the one directly responsible.
20. No executive or employee should ever be required, or expected, to be at the same time an assistant to, and critic of, another.
21. Any executive whose work is subject to regular inspection should, wherever practicable, be given the assistance and facilities necessary to enable him to maintain an independent check of the quality of his work.

MINI-TEXT IN SUPERVISION, ADMINISTRATION, MANAGEMENT, AND ORGANIZATION

I. Brief Highlights

Listed concisely and sequentially are major headings and important data in the field for quick recall and review.

A. Levels of Management
Any organization of some size has several levels of management. In terms of a ladder, the levels are:

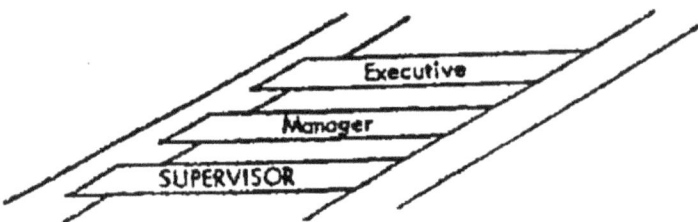

The first level is very important because it is the beginning point of management leadership.

B. What the Supervisor Must Learn
A supervisor must learn to:
1. Deal with people and their differences
2. Get the job done through people
3. Recognize the problems when they exist
4. Overcome obstacles to good performance
5. Evaluate the performance of people
6. Check his own performance in terms of accomplishment

C. A Definition of Supervisor
The term supervisor means any individual having authority, in the interests of the employer, to hire, transfer, suspend, lay-off, recall, promote, discharge, assign, reward, or discipline other employees or responsibility to direct them, or to adjust their grievances, or effectively to recommend such action, if, in connection with the foregoing, exercise of such authority is not of a merely routine or clerical nature but requires the use of independent judgment.

D. Elements of the Team Concept
What is involved in teamwork? The component parts are:
1. Members
2. A leader
3. Goals
4. Plans
5. Cooperation
6. Spirit

E. Principles of Organization
1. A team member must know what his job is.
2. Be sure that the nature and scope of a job are understood.
3. Authority and responsibility should be carefully spelled out.
4. A supervisor should be permitted to make the maximum number of decisions affecting his employees.
5. Employees should report to only one supervisor.
6. A supervisor should direct only as many employees as he can handle effectively.
7. An organization plan should be flexible.

8. Inspection and performance of work should be separate.
9. Organizational problems should receive immediate attention.
10. Assign work in line with ability and experience.

F. The Four Important Parts of Every Job
1. Inherent in every job is the *accountability* for results.
2. A second set of factors in every job is *responsibilities*.
3. Along with duties and responsibilities one must have the *authority* to act within certain limits without obtaining permission to proceed.
4. No job exists in a vacuum. The supervisor is surrounded by key *relationships*.

G. Principles of Delegation
Where work is delegated for the first time, the supervisor should think in terms of these questions:
1. Who is best qualified to do this?
2. Can an employee improve his abilities by doing this?
3. How long should an employee spend on this?
4. Are there any special problems for which he will need guidance?
5. How broad a delegation can I make?

H. Principles of Effective Communications
1. Determine the media.
2. To whom directed?
3. Identification and source authority.
4. Is communication understood?

I. Principles of Work Improvement
1. Most people usually do only the work which is assigned to them.
2. Workers are likely to fit assigned work into the time available to perform it.
3. A good workload usually stimulates output.
4. People usually do their best work when they know that results will be reviewed or inspected.
5. Employees usually feel that someone else is responsible for conditions of work, workplace layout, job methods, type of tools/equipment, and other such factors.
6. Employees are usually defensive about their job security.
7. Employees have natural resistance to change.
8. Employees can support or destroy a supervisor.
9. A supervisor usually earns the respect of his people through his personal example of diligence and efficiency.

J. Areas of Job Improvement
The areas of job improvement are quite numerous, but the most common ones which a supervisor can identify and utilize are:
1. Departmental layout
2. Flow of work
3. Workplace layout
4. Utilization of manpower
5. Work methods
6. Materials handling

7. Utilization
8. Motion economy

K. Seven Key Points in Making Improvements
   1. Select the job to be improved
   2. Study how it is being done now
   3. Question the present method
   4. Determine actions to be taken
   5. Chart proposed method
   6. Get approval and apply
   7. Solicit worker participation

l. Corrective Techniques of Job Improvement
   Specific Problems
   1. Size of workload
   2. Inability to meet schedules
   3. Strain and fatigue
   4. Improper use of men and skills
   5. Waste, poor quality, unsafe conditions
   6. Bottleneck conditions that hinder output
   7. Poor utilization of equipment and machine
   8. Efficiency and productivity of labor

   General Improvement
   1. Departmental layout
   2. Flow of work
   3. Work plan layout
   4. Utilization of manpower
   5. Work methods
   6. Materials handling
   7. Utilization of equipment
   8. Motion economy

   Corrective Techniques
   1. Study with scale model
   2. Flow chart study
   3. Motion analysis
   4. Comparison of units produced to standard allowance
   5. Methods analysis
   6. Flow chart and equipment study
   7. Down time vs. running time
   8. Motion analysis

M. A Planning Checklist
   1. Objectives
   2. Controls
   3. Delegations
   4. Communications
   5. Resources
   6. Manpower

7. Equipment
8. Supplies and materials
9. Utilization of time
10. Safety
11. Money
12. Work
13. Timing of improvements

N. Five Characteristics of Good Directions
In order to get results, directions must be:
1. Possible of accomplishment
2. Agreeable with worker interests
3. Related to mission
4. Planned and complete
5. Unmistakably clear

O. Types of Directions
1. Demands or direct orders
2. Requests
3. Suggestion or implication
4. volunteering

P. Controls
A typical listing of the overall areas in which the supervisor should establish controls might be:
1. Manpower
2. Materials
3. Quality of work
4. Quantity of work
5. Time
6. Space
7. Money
8. Methods

Q. Orienting the New Employee
1. Prepare for him
2. Welcome the new employee
3. Orientation for the job
4. Follow-up

R. Checklist for Orienting New Employees   Yes   No
1. Do you appreciate the feelings of new employees
   when they first report for work?   ___   ___
2. Are you aware of the fact that the new employee must
   make a big adjustment to his job?   ___   ___
3. Have you given him good reasons for liking the job and
   the organization?   ___   ___
4. Have you prepared for his first day on the job?   ___   ___
5. Did you welcome him cordially and make him feel needed?   ___   ___

	Yes	No
6. Did you establish rapport with him so that he feels free to talk and discuss matters with you?	___	___
7. Did you explain his job to him and his relationship to you?	___	___
8. Does he know that his work will be evaluated periodically on a basis that is fair and objective?	___	___
9. Did you introduce him to his fellow workers in such a way that they are likely to accept him?	___	___
10. Does he know what employee benefits he will receive?	___	___
11. Does he understand the importance of being on the job and what to do if he must leave his duty station?	___	___
12. Has he been impressed with the importance of accident prevention and safe practice?	___	___
13. Does he generally know his way around the department?	___	___
14. Is he under the guidance of a sponsor who will teach the right way of doing things?	___	___
15. Do you plan to follow-up so that he will continue to adjust successfully to his job?	___	___

S. Principles of Learning
   1. Motivation
   2. Demonstration or explanation
   3. Practice

T. Causes of Poor Performance
   1. Improper training for job
   2. Wrong tools
   3. Inadequate directions
   4. Lack of supervisory follow-up
   5. Poor communications
   6. Lack of standards of performance
   7. Wrong work habits
   8. Low morale
   9. Other

U. Four Major Steps in On-The-Job Instruction
   1. Prepare the worker
   2. Present the operation
   3. Tryout performance
   4. Follow-up

V. Employees Want Five Things
   1. Security
   2. Opportunity
   3. Recognition
   4. Inclusion
   5. Expression

W. Some Don'ts in Regard to Praise
1. Don't praise a person for something he hasn't done.
2. Don't praise a person unless you can be sincere.
3. Don't be sparing in praise just because your superior withholds it from you.
4. Don't let too much time elapse between good performance and recognition of it

X. How to Gain Your Workers' Confidence
Methods of developing confidence include such things as:
1. Knowing the interests, habits, hobbies of employees
2. Admitting your own inadequacies
3. Sharing and telling of confidence in others
4. Supporting people when they are in trouble
5. Delegating matters that can be well handled
6. Being frank and straightforward about problems and working conditions
7. Encouraging others to bring their problems to you
8. Taking action on problems which impede worker progress

Y. Sources of Employee Problems
On-the-job causes might be such things as:
1. A feeling that favoritism is exercised in assignments
2. Assignment of overtime
3. An undue amount of supervision
4. Changing methods or systems
5. Stealing of ideas or trade secrets
6. Lack of interest in job
7. Threat of reduction in force
8. Ignorance or lack of communications
9. Poor equipment
10. Lack of knowing how supervisor feels toward employee
11. Shift assignments

Off-the-job problems might have to do with:
1. Health
2. Finances
3. Housing
4. Family

Z. The Supervisor's Key to Discipline
There are several key points about discipline which the supervisor should keep in mind:
1. Job discipline is one of the disciplines of life and is directed by the supervisor.
2. It is more important to correct an employee fault than to fix blame for it.
3. Employee performance is affected by problems both on the job and off.
4. Sudden or abrupt changes in behavior can be indications of important employee problems.
5. Problems should be dealt with as soon as possible after they are identified.
6. The attitude of the supervisor may have more to do with solving problems than the techniques of problem solving.
7. Correction of employee behavior should be resorted to only after the supervisor is sure that training or counseling will not be helpful.

12

8. Be sure to document your disciplinary actions.
9. Make sure that you are disciplining on the basis of facts rather than personal feelings.
10. Take each disciplinary step in order, being careful not to make snap judgments, or decisions based on impatience.

AA. Five Important Processes of Management
1. Planning
2. Organizing
3. Scheduling
4. Controlling
5. Motivating

BB. When the Supervisor Fails to Plan
1. Supervisor creates impression of not knowing his job
2. May lead to excessive overtime
3. Job runs itself—supervisor lacks control
4. Deadlines and appointments missed
5. Parts of the work go undone
6. Work interrupted by emergencies
7. Sets a bad example
8. Uneven workload creates peaks and valleys
9. Too much time on minor details at expense of more important tasks

CC. Fourteen General Principles of Management
1. Division of work
2. Authority and responsibility
3. Discipline
4. Unity of command
5. Unity of direction
6. Subordination of individual interest to general interest
7. Remuneration of personnel
8. Centralization
9. Scalar chain
10. Order
11. Equity
12. Stability of tenure of personnel
13. Initiative
14. Esprit de corps

DD. Change

Bringing about change is perhaps attempted more often, and yet less well understood, than anything else the supervisor does. How do people generally react to change? (People tend to resist change that is imposed upon them by other individuals or circumstances.

Change is characteristic of every situation. It is a part of every real endeavor where the efforts of people are concerned.

1. Why do people resist change?
   People may resist change because of:
   a. Fear of the unknown
   b. Implied criticism
   c. Unpleasant experiences in the past
   d. Fear of loss of status
   e. Threat to the ego
   f. Fear of loss of economic stability

2. How can we best overcome the resistance to change?
   In initiating change, take these steps:
   a. Get ready to sell
   b. Identify sources of help
   c. Anticipate objections
   d. Sell benefits
   e. Listen in depth
   f. Follow up

II. Brief Topical Summaries

   A. Who/What is the Supervisor?
      1. The supervisor is often called the "highest level employee and the lowest level manager."
      2. A supervisor is a member of both management and the work group. He acts as a bridge between the two.
      3. Most problems in supervision are in the area of human relations, or people problems.
      4. Employees expect: Respect, opportunity to learn and to advance, and a sense of belonging, and so forth.
      5. Supervisors are responsible for directing people and organizing work. Planning is of paramount importance.
      6. A position description is a set of duties and responsibilities inherent to a given position.
      7. It is important to keep the position description up-to-date and to provide each employee with his own copy.

   B. The Sociology of Work
      1. People are alike in many ways; however, each individual is unique.
      2. The supervisor is challenged in getting to know employee differences. Acquiring skills in evaluating individuals is an asset.
      3. Maintaining meaningful working relationships in the organization is of great importance.
      4. The supervisor has an obligation to help individuals to develop to their fullest potential.
      5. Job rotation on a planned basis helps to build versatility and to maintain interest and enthusiasm in work groups.
      6. Cross training (job rotation) provides backup skills.

7. The supervisor can help reduce tension by maintaining a sense of humor, providing guidance to employees, and by making reasonable and timely decisions. Employees respond favorably to working under reasonably predictable circumstances.
8. Change is characteristic of all managerial behavior. The supervisor must adjust to changes in procedures, new methods, technological changes, and to a number of new and sometimes challenging situations.
9. To overcome the natural tendency for people to resist change, the supervisor should become more skillful in initiating change.

C. Principles and Practices of Supervision
1. Employees should be required to answer to only one superior.
2. A supervisor can effectively direct only a limited number of employees, depending upon the complexity, variety, and proximity of the jobs involved.
3. The organizational chart presents the organization in graphic form. It reflects lines of authority and responsibility as well as interrelationships of units within the organization.
4. Distribution of work can be improved through an analysis using the "Work Distribution Chart."
5. The "Work Distribution Chart" reflects the division of work within a unit in understandable form.
6. When related tasks are given to an employee, he has a better chance of increasing his skills through training.
7. The individual who is given the responsibility for tasks must also be given the appropriate authority to insure adequate results.
8. The supervisor should delegate repetitive, routine work. Preparation of recurring reports, maintaining leave and attendance records are some examples.
9. Good discipline is essential to good task performance. Discipline is reflected in the actions of employees on the job in the absence of supervision.
10. Disciplinary action may have to be taken when the positive aspects of discipline have failed. Reprimand, warning, and suspension are examples of disciplinary action.
11. If a situation calls for a reprimand, be sure it is deserved and remember it is to be done in private.

D. Dynamic Leadership
1. A style is a personal method or manner of exerting influence.
2. Authoritarian leaders often see themselves as the source of power and authority.
3. The democratic leader often perceives the group as the source of authority and power.
4. Supervisors tend to do better when using the pattern of leadership that is most natural for them.
5. Social scientists suggest that the effective supervisor use the leadership style that best fits the problem or circumstances involved.
6. All four styles—telling, selling, consulting, joining—have their place. Using one does not preclude using the other at another time.

7. The theory X point of view assumes that the average person dislikes work, will avoid it whenever possible, and must be coerced to achieve organizational objectives.
8. The theory Y point of view assumes that the average person considers work to be a natural as play, and, when the individual is committed, he requires little supervision or direction to accomplish desired objectives.
9. The leader's basic assumptions concerning human behavior and human nature affect his actions, decisions, and other managerial practices.
10. Dissatisfaction among employees is often present, but difficult to isolate. The supervisor should seek to weaken dissatisfaction by keeping promises, being sincere and considerate, keeping employees informed, and so forth.
11. Constructive suggestions should be encouraged during the natural progress of the work.

E. Processes for Solving Problems
1. People find their daily tasks more meaningful and satisfying when they can improve them.
2. The causes of problems, or the key factors, are often hidden in the background. Ability to solve problems often involves the ability to isolate them from their backgrounds. There is some substance to the cliché that some persons "can't see the forest for the trees."
3. New procedures are often developed from old ones. Problems should be broken down into manageable parts. New ideas can be adapted from old one.
4. People think differently in problem-solving situations. Using a logical, patterned approach is often useful. One approach found to be useful includes these steps:
    a. Define the problem
    b. Establish objectives
    c. Get the facts
    d. Weigh and decide
    e. Take action
    f. Evaluate action

F. Training for Results
1. Participants respond best when they feel training is important to them.
2. The supervisor has responsibility for the training and development of those who report to him.
3. When training is delegated to others, great care must be exercised to insure the trainer has knowledge, aptitude, and interest for his work as a trainer.
4. Training (learning) of some type goes on continually. The most successful supervisor makes certain the learning contributes in a productive manner to operational goals.
5. New employees are particularly susceptible to training. Older employees facing new job situations require specific training, as well as having need for development and growth opportunities.
6. Training needs require continuous monitoring.
7. The training officer of an agency is a professional with a responsibility to assist supervisors in solving training problems.

8. Many of the self-development steps important to the supervisor's own growth are equally important to the development of peers and subordinates. Knowledge of these is important when the supervisor consults with others on development and growth opportunities.

G. Health, Safety, and Accident Prevention
1. Management-minded supervisors take appropriate measures to assist employees in maintaining health and in assuring safe practices in the work environment.
2. Effective safety training and practices help to avoid injury and accidents.
3. Safety should be a management goal. All infractions of safety which are observed should be corrected without exception.
4. Employees' safety attitude, training and instruction, provision of safe tools and equipment, supervision, and leadership are considered highly important factors which contribute to safety and which can be influenced directly by supervisors.
5. When accidents do occur, they should be investigated promptly for very important reasons, including the fact that information which is gained can be used to prevent accidents in the future.

H. Equal Employment Opportunity
1. The supervisor should endeavor to treat all employees fairly, without regard to religion, race, sex, or national origin.
2. Groups tend to reflect the attitude of the leader. Prejudice can be detected even in very subtle form. Supervisors must strive to create a feeling of mutual respect and confidence in every employee.
3. Complete utilization of all human resources is a national goal. Equitable consideration should be accorded women in the work force, minority-group members, the physically and mentally handicapped, and the older employee. The important question is: "Who can do the job?"
4. Training opportunities, recognition for performance, overtime assignments, promotional opportunities, and all other personnel actions are to be handled on an equitable basis.

I. Improving Communications
1. Communications is achieving understanding between the sender and the receiver of a message. It also means sharing information—the creation of understanding.
2. Communication is basic to all human activity. Words are means of conveying meanings; however, real meanings are in people.
3. There are very practical differences in the effectiveness of one-way, impersonal, and two-way communications. Words spoken face-to-face are better understood. Telephone conversations are effective, but lack the rapport of person-to-person exchanges. The whole person communicates.
4. Cooperation and communication in an organization go hand in hand. When there is a mutual respect between people, spelling out rules and procedures for communicating is unnecessary.
5. There are several barriers to effective communications. These include failure to listen with respect and understanding, lack of skill in feedback, and misinterpreting the meanings of words used by the speaker. It is also common

practice to listen to what we want to hear, and tune out things we do not want to hear.
6. Communication is management's chief problem. The supervisor should accept the challenge to communicate more effectively and to improve interagency and intra-agency communications.
7. The supervisor may often plan for and conduct meetings. The planning phase is critical and may determine the success or the failure of a meeting.
8. Speaking before groups usually requires extra effort. Stage fright may never disappear completely, but it can be controlled.

J. Self-Development
1. Every employee is responsible for his own self-development.
2. Toastmaster and toastmistress clubs offer opportunities to improve skills in oral communications.
3. Planning for one's own self-development is of vital importance. Supervisors know their own strengths and limitations better than anyone else.
4. Many opportunities are open to aid the supervisor in his developmental efforts, including job assignments; training opportunities, both governmental and non-governmental—to include universities and professional conferences and seminars.
5. Programmed instruction offers a means of studying at one's own rate.
6. Where difficulties may arise from a supervisor's being away from his work for training, he may participate in televised home study or correspondence courses to meet his self-development needs.

K. Teaching and Training
1. The Teaching Process
Teaching is encouraging and guiding the learning activities of students toward established goals. In most cases this process consists of five steps: preparation, presentation, summarization, evaluation, and application.

   a. Preparation
   Preparation is two-fold in nature; that of the supervisor and the employee. Preparation by the supervisor is absolutely essential to success. He must know what, when, where, how, and whom he will teach. Some of the factors that should be considered are:
   1) The objectives
   2) The materials needed
   3) The methods to be used
   4) Employee participation
   5) Employee interest
   6) Training aids
   7) Evaluation
   8) Summarization

   Employee preparation consists in preparing the employee to receive the material. Probably the most important single factor in the preparation of the employee is arousing and maintaining his interest. He must know the objectives of the training, why he is there, how the material can be used, and its importance to him.

b. Presentation
In presentation, have a carefully designed plan and follow it. The plan should be accurate and complete, yet flexible enough to meet situations as they arise. The method of presentation will be determined by the particular situation and objectives.

c. Summary
A summary should be made at the end of every training unit and program. In addition, there may be internal summaries depending on the nature of the material being taught. The important thing is that the trainee must always be able to understand how each part of the new material relates to the whole.

d. Application
The supervisor must arrange work so the employee will be given a chance to apply new knowledge or skills while the material is still clear in his mind and interest is high. The trainee does not really know whether he has learned the material until he has been given a chance to apply it. If the material is not applied, it loses most of its value.

e. Evaluation
The purpose of all training is to promote learning. To determine whether the training has been a success or failure, the supervisor must evaluate this learning.
In the broadest sense, evaluation includes all the devices, methods, skills, and techniques used by the supervisor to keep himself and the employees informed as to their progress toward the objectives they are pursuing. The extent to which the employee has mastered the knowledge, skills, and abilities, or changed his attitudes, as determined by the program objectives, is the extent to which instruction has succeeded or failed.
Evaluation should not be confined to the end of the lesson, day, or program but should be used continuously. We shall note later the way this relates to the rest of the teaching process.

2. Teaching Methods
A teaching method is a pattern of identifiable student and instructor activity used in presenting training material.
All supervisors are faced with the problem of deciding which method should be used at a given time.

a. Lecture
The lecture is direct oral presentation of material by the supervisor. The present trend is to place less emphasis on the trainer's activity and more on that of the trainee.

b. Discussion
Teaching by discussion or conference involves using questions and other techniques to arouse interest and focus attention upon certain areas, and by doing so creating a learning situation. This can be one of the most

valuable methods because it gives the employees an opportunity to express their ideas and pool their knowledge.

    c. Demonstration
The demonstration is used to teach how something works or how to do something. It can be used to show a principle or what the results of a series of actions will be. A well-staged demonstration is particularly effective because it shows proper methods of performance in a realistic manner.

    d. Performance
Performance is one of the most fundamental of all learning techniques or teaching methods. The trainee may be able to tell how a specific operation should be performed but he cannot be sure he knows how to perform the operation until he has done so.
As with all methods, there are certain advantages and disadvantages to each method.

    e. Which Method to Use
Moreover, there are other methods and techniques of teaching. It is difficult to use any method without other methods entering into it. In any learning situation, a combination of methods is usually more effective than any one method alone.

Finally, evaluation must be integrated into the other aspects of the teaching-learning process.

It must be used in the motivation of the trainees; it must be used to assist in developing understanding during the training; and it must be related to employee application of the results of training.

This is distinctly the role of the supervisor.

www.ingramcontent.com/pod-product-compliance
Lightning Source LLC
Chambersburg PA
CBHW080734230426
43665CB00020B/2735